Our Lady and the Church

OUR LADY

AND THE

CHURCH

Hugo Rahner, s.j.

Translated by
Sebastian Bullough, o.p.

ZACCHEUS PRESS
Bethesda

Imprimi Potest:	Fr. Hilarius Carpenter, O.P.
	Prior Provincialias Provinciae
	Angliae Ord. Praed.
	January 20, 1958
Nihil Obstat:	Joannes M.T. Barton, S.T.D., L.S.S.
	Censor deputatus
Imprimatur:	E. Morrogh Bernard
	Vicar General, Westminster
	November 12, 1960

Grateful acknowledgment is made to Darton, Longman and Todd Ltd for permission to reproduce the translation.

ZACCHEUS PRESS and the colophon are trademarks of Zaccheus Press.

The Zaccheus Press colophon was designed by Michelle Dick.

Library of Congress Cataloging-in-Publication Data

Rahner, Hugo, 1900-1968.
  [Maria und die Kirche. English]
  Our Lady and the church / by Hugo Rahner ; translated by Sebastian Bullough.
    p. cm.
  ISBN 0-9725981-1-1 (pbk. : alk. paper)
  1. Mary, Blessed Virgin, Saint—Meditations. I. Title.
  BX2160.23.R3413 2004
  232.91—dc22

                                        2004024721

10 9 8 7 6 5 4 3 2

To learn more, please visit our webpage:

www.zaccheuspress.com

CONTENTS

FOREWORD

THERE is, perhaps, a particular relevance attaching to the lines of thought presented in this volume when the Church has recently proclaimed, with all her teaching authority, that the doctrine of the Assumption of our Lady is indeed a revealed dogma of the faith. All over Christendom men have been asking themselves what is the precise place of this dogma in the body of Catholic Truth, and furthermore what is its special significance for the development of our spiritual lives?

The most important formative element in Catholic piety today is probably the newly-found understanding of the lifegiving power of our holy mother the Church in her sacraments and her liturgy. But at the same time there have been during the last hundred years such remarkable dogmatic developments, bringing out ever more clearly the place of our Lady in the system of Catholic thought. Now there are some Christians—including profound thinkers and earnestly striving souls—who feel that these two trends are in contradiction: perhaps their eyes are still "held" (Luke 24:16), so that they cannot yet recognize the heavenly mystery when they look at the earthly features of the Church, and it is not yet granted to them to see in the simple earthly life of Mary the Mother of God the highest mystery of all the Bible and theology, in the birth of God from a human virgin the very nature of the Church, and in the mystery of the Church itself the profoundest element in our spiritual formation.

It is the purpose of this book to collect and unite these ideas. We must learn to see the Church in our Lady, and in our Lady the Church. The two mysteries are most intimately connected, and a deeper understanding of both together will bring us to realize better the meaning of grace in our souls and progress in the spiritual life.

The eleven chapters of this book deal with the spiritual life, and are entirely based upon the wisdom of the Fathers of the Church, who indeed have so much to teach us today about the principles of the spiritual life, and who can remind us of many things which since the days of the early Church have either been forgotten or become obscured. The early Christians' devotion to Mother Church always went hand-in-hand with their devotion to the Mother of God, and this was because they still realized that the whole mystery as presented in the Scriptures shows Mary, the virgin mother, to be essentially the symbol of the Church, our mother. The whole life of our

Lady, from her Immaculate Conception to her glorious Assumption, thus appears as a symbol of the whole life of the Church and of our own spiritual lives. The history of the Church begins in the womb of the Virgin Mary, and within the Church is the fulfilment of our own and the world's eternal vocation, when the divine Redeemer lifted the curse from fallen nature. How profound are the enigmatic words of the Syrian Father, Saint Ephrem:

> Mother Earth it was that bore all flesh, and was accursed. But for the sake of the flesh that is the Church incorruptible, this fleshly earth was blessed from the beginning, for Mary was the Mother Earth that brought the Church to birth.[1]

When therefore in our own time the Holy Father Pope Pius XII proclaims in the presence of the whole Church that the body of the virgin mother, from which God was born, was taken up to heaven, it is no more than a confirmation of the doctrine of the Church previously given in the encyclical on the Mystical Body of Christ. And we might here summarize the thought of the pages that follow in a single quotation from a medieval mystic who was still steeped in the spirit of Augustine and the early Church.

> Christ is one, and one alone: head and body. He is one: Son of the one Father in heaven, son of the one Mother on earth: two sonships, but one son. The head and members are more than one, yet one

son: so Mary and the Church are two, yet one single mother, two virgins and yet one. Each is mother, each is virgin. Both conceived by the same Spirit, without human seed. Both bore to God the Father a child unblemished. The one, without sin, gave birth to Christ's body, the other restored His body through the power of the remission of sins. Both are the Mother of Christ, but neither can bring Him to birth without the other.

Thus it is that in the inspired Scriptures, what is said in the widest sense of the Virgin Mother the Church, is said in a special sense of the Virgin Mary. And what is spoken of the Virgin Mother Mary in a personal way, can rightly be applied in a general way to the Virgin Mother the Church.

But every faithful soul is in a sense the bride of the Word of God, the Mother of Christ, His daughter and His sister, virgin yet a mother. And moreover whatever is said of God's eternal wisdom itself, can be applied in a wide sense to the Church, in a narrower sense to Mary, and in a particular way to every faithful soul.[2]

HUGO RAHNER, S.J.

Innsbruck

Our Lady

and the

Church

Chapter One

An Introduction:
Mary Essentially a
Symbol of the Church

When we come to look at the development of piety during the last half-century, a development to which every one of us has in some way contributed, we must come to the conclusion that two main trends are distinguishable: ours is undoubtedly an age of a reawakening of men's love for the Church as their mother; and at the same time it has been the witness of a remarkable development of the Church's teaching about our Lady. *Mater Ecclesia* and *Mater Christi*, Ecclesiology and Mariology: these are the two ways in which so many are today drawing closer to Christ.

It was indeed with no exaggeration that Romano Guardini wrote prophetically in 1922:

A new religious movement has begun, whose effects will be far-reaching beyond measure: souls have become aware of the Church....

The very fact of the Church has become a living power. We are beginning to understand that the Church is everything. We begin to feel what the Saints felt, when they spoke so passionately in her defense. Did not their words sometimes seem to us but empty phrases? But now it is different. The philosopher will come to see in the Church the final and conclusive answer to his earnest search for the roots of all reality. The artist will come to find in her powerful beauty the fulfilment of his restless seeking for complete perfection of form. The moralist will find that she possesses complete perfection of life, when all human striving is sanctified in Christ, when all right and wrong become plain, and the Kingdom of God ultimately prevails. The politician (in the proper sense of him who seeks the public good) will come to realize that she has the answer to the problem of social order and of every man's fulfilment of his vocation in society.[3]

This love of the Church, which we are even going to call "Devotion to the Church," has indeed grown and matured over the years, especially in men's attitude to the Sacraments and liturgical prayer: the growth has been slow perhaps, but showing a steady increase. But today we feel we are on certain ground, when we speak of the mystery of the Church in the terms of Saint Paul and the Fathers, since Pius XII's encyclical *Mystici Corporis*.

At first sight the strong Marian movement of our day seems to have little connection with this theology of the Church, and even perhaps to run counter to it.

It has seemed to some to involve dogmatic declarations almost as it were for their own sakes, an artificial pressing into dogmatic form of beliefs long current in Catholic thought, a part of a tendency to fit everything into a dogmatic framework. Of course the newly proclaimed dogmas are accepted in the full spirit of obedience, but it has for some remained a problem to see their proper place in the structure of today's rapidly developing piety. It has not always been easy to fit together the somewhat subjective Marian piety, beginning with the Rosary and extending to the question of our Lady's universal mediation of graces and the devotion to her immaculate heart, with the essentially objective sacramental and liturgical piety involved in "Devotion to the Church."

But there cannot be any contradiction. We know that the Church in the development of her piety is guided by the Holy Spirit, and we therefore know that our devotion to our Mother the Church cannot possibly run counter to our devotion to the Mother of God. Yet it cannot be denied that many earnest Christians somehow feel that there is some contradiction, and this is probably due to an over-enthusiastic devotion to one or the other aspect, with a corresponding dry lack of feeling towards the other.

It is to attempt to resolve this tension that this book has been written. It has one single object: to show from the warm-hearted theology of the great Fathers and Doctors that the whole mystery of the Church is inseparably bound up with the mystery of Mary. We need to learn once more what was so treasured by the early Church: to learn to see the Church in our Lady, and our Lady in the Church. The result of this attitude will be an ever joyful readiness to accept whatever may come in dogmatic developments about our Lady, and at the same time a consequent deepening of our understanding of the nature of the Church. And the Spirit of God, which overshadowed Mary (Luke 1:35), and descended on her with the infant Church at Pentecost (Acts 1:14), will bless this attitude, and Pius XII's words about our Lady at the end of his encyclical on the Mystical Body will bear fruit:

> It was the powerful intercession of Mary that obtained that the Spirit of the Divine Redeemer, already poured out on the Cross, should be bestowed at Pentecost with wonderful gifts upon the infant Church. It was she who was there to tend the Mystical Body of Christ, born of the Savior's pierced Heart, with the same motherly care that she spent on the Child Jesus in the crib.

Let us begin by stating the fundamental truth, which is the basis of all that is to follow, and lies at the root of the early Christians' teaching about the Church and love of the Church: Mary, the mother of Jesus, in virtue of the ineffable dignity of being the Virgin Mother of God made Man, became the essential symbol of the Church, our Mother. Or we could put it the other way round: because the merciful Father saw in her the essential instrument of salvation for all "who are born not of the blood, nor of the will of the flesh, nor of the will of man, but of God" (John 1:13), Mary became the Virgin Mother of God.[4]

One of the basic elements of the theology of the Church, found at the beginning in the Revelation of John, and then through the early Fathers, Justin, Irenaeus and Hippolytus, onwards through Augustine to the *Summa* of Aquinas, is the idea of the Church as the "Mother of the Living." This idea is linked with that of Eve, as the first mother of the living, and in turn receives fulfilment in Mary giving birth to the living God. Eve, Mary and the Church: for the early theologians these three formed but one picture with three transparencies.

Mary owes her position as the second Eve and Mother of God's new human race to her dignity as Mother of God; and similarly the Church owes her position to the fact of her being the mother of the Mystical Body of Christ, the mediatrix of divine life and virgin mother of all men whose life is in Christ. "As Mary gave birth to Him who is your head, so the Church gives birth to you. For the Church also is both mother and virgin: mother in the womb of our love, virgin in her inviolate faith. She is the mother of many nations who yet are one body and are thus likened to that one Virgin Mary, the mother of many but yet of the one," in the words of Augustine.[5]

But we can go deeper into these fundamental notions. In Patristic thought Mary is the *typos* of the Church: symbol, central idea, and as it were summary of all that is meant by the Church in her nature and vocation.

And here we should remind ourselves of what theology since Saint Paul has meant by typology. From the first instant of grace God's plan of Redemption has looked forward, undistracted by sin or betrayal, towards one thing: the Incarnation of the Word and the salvation of mankind; in other words, towards Christ and the Church. Every detail therefore of the long story leading to this, has a significance—indeed a prime significance—that points this way. "For in Him were all things created," says Saint Paul (Colossians 1:16) speaking of Christ, "the firstborn of every creature" (Colossians 1:15).

The typological content of the characters of Old Testament history is their relationship to Christ and to His body, that is to ourselves. All that happened to the chosen people was "done in a figure of us... upon whom the ends of the world are come" (1 Corinthians 10:6, 11). Adam, the first man, is quite simply the "figure of Him who was to come" (Romans 5:14). The whole typology of the Old Testament points to Christ, but not only to Him in His life from Bethlehem to Golgotha, but by Him and through Him to the "last times" when Christ is building up His Mystical Body, and finally to the events of the Parousia, when Christ "will reform the body of our lowness, made like to the body of His glory... and you also shall appear with Him in glory" (Philippians 3:21 and Colossians 3:4).

Into this typological plan of Christ and His Church,

the early theologians would also place Mary, the human mother of the Word made flesh. She is also "the type of what is to come," for it was her *Fiat* that marks the end of the Old Testament: she now saw what prophets and kings desired to see, and in her womb the New Testament begins, the kingdom of the true David, of whose "kingdom there shall be no end" (Luke 1:33). She is the Queen of Patriarchs and of Prophets, and the Queen of Apostles. Past and future meet in her: all the light of the Old Testament, from Eve to the Book of Wisdom, shines in her, for the sun of justice entered into her womb.

For the Roman theologian Hippolytus at the end of the second century, Mary appears as the last of the prophets. Anointed prophets and anointed kings longed to see the Messias, the Lord's anointed; and she received Him into her womb: "The Blessed Virgin Mary, who had longed for this too, conceived the Word in her womb."[6]

But here also is the idea of the Church, "the bride of Christ," the new Eve stepping forth from the godless desert, fragrant with the anointing of God's grace. The Old finds its end in her, and the New finds its beginning: "for the Logos, born from all eternity, redeems the firstformed Adam in the Virgin's womb."[7]

Thus the early Church saw Mary and the Church as a single figure: type and antitype form one print as seal and wax. And Irenaeus of Lyons, whose thought derives from Polycarp, the disciple of John, and therefore directly from the heart of Christ Himself, sees in the words of the angel to our Lady a prophecy of the Church's kingdom to come (Luke 1:33):

Who else reigns in the house of Jacob forever, but Christ Jesus our Lord, Son of the most High? He gave His promise in the Law and the Prophets, that He would make manifest His salvation to all flesh: for this He became a Son of Man, that man might become a Son of God. Therefore Mary rejoiced, and speaking prophetically in the Church's name, said "My soul doth magnify the Lord." All is renewed, when the Word newly made flesh begins the task of winning back to God mankind who had strayed so far from God.[8]

The Virgin's Magnificat is for Irenaeus a song of prophecy: she sang it in the hill-country of Judea, where she is a type of the Church to come, which still lay hidden within her. The song she sang in her ecstasy was a song of the Church, fulfilling the promise "to Abraham and to his seed forever": Adam's race brought back to God in her Son, Adam redeemed in her womb. Hippolytus, disciple of Irenaeus, speaks of the last blessing that the dying Moses gave to his people:

Moses said: "Through God's blessing his land shall remain his own, and be blessed with the dew of heaven" (cf. Deuteronomy 33:13). This was said of Mary, who was the blessed land, and the Word was made flesh, coming down as the dew. But it can also be said of the Church, for she is blest by the Lord as a holy land and a paradise of bliss, and the

dew is the Lord, the Redeemer Himself. For this holy
land has inherited all the Lord's blessings from the
holy House, from the virginal birth, as these latter
ages have shown.[9]

Here again Mary and the Church are seen as one, for
the Church had its beginning in her womb, and from
her virginal earth the kingdom of God has blossomed.

At the end of the second century a Christian in
Phrygia named Abercius had an inscription engraved
on his tombstone, which is now to be seen in the Lateran
Museum in Rome and which includes a deeply symbolic
phrase. "The Faith," it runs,

> has ever been my guide, and has given me to eat a
> fish, a great and pure fish, which a spotless virgin
> drew forth from the well.

It has been much discussed whether this refers to
our Lady or to the Church, who gives to us the sacred
fish, symbol of Christ the eucharistic food. But surely
we have here type and antitype in one: it is the one
Christ, to whom Mary gave birth and who is given to
us by the Church. The symbol begins with Mary and is
fulfilled in the Church. Thus also Saint Ephrem the
Syrian, who was heir to the whole Mariology of the
early Church, sings in a song of praise of the Church:

> Blessed art thou, O Church, for of thee Isaiah
> speaks in his prophetic song of joy: Behold a virgin
> shall conceive and bear a son: O hidden mystery of
> the Church![10]

So also Ambrose refers the words of the canticle to Mary, as she sings the Magnificat, hastening through the hill-country of Judea, and at the same time to the Church striding through the hills of the centuries.

> Watch Mary, my children, for the word prophetically uttered of the Church, applies to her also: "How lovely thy sandalled steps, O princely maid!"
>
> Yes, princely and lovely indeed are the Church's steps, as she goes to announce her Gospel of joy: lovely the steps of Mary and the Church![11]

And the holy monk Anastasius of Sinai sees the *Ave Maria* as spoken to the Church: "Blessed art thou among women, hail, our life, thou lifegiving Mother of the faithful, hail, holy Church, Mother of Christ, blessed is the fruit of thy womb, the one people from all the nations of the world."[12] This penetration of symbols often caused Mary to be simply called "the Church." For instance in the course of the controversy between Archelaus and Manes, which belongs to the fourth century, when the heretic is attacking Mary's virginity, he speaks of her as "the chaste and most pure virgin Church," evidently using a phrase that was current at the time.[13]

And Cyril of Alexandria at the end of his wonderful sermon on our Lady at the Council of Ephesus in 431 speaks with enthusiasm:

> And so, brethren, may it be granted to us to adore with deep humility the indivisible Trinity. And then let us praise with songs of joy Mary ever

virgin, who herself is clearly the holy Church, together with her Son and most chaste spouse. To God be praise forever.[14]

And finally, the Anglo-Saxon Bede can express in a word what we shall examine more closely later on, when he speaks of the Church simply as *Dei Genitrix Ecclesia*.[15]

Thus we find ourselves at the heart of the early Church's teaching about our Lady and the Church. This is the fundamental doctrine, that Mary is a type or symbol of the Church, and therefore everything that we find in the Gospel about Mary can be understood in a proper biblical sense of the mystery of the Church. And indeed it can be said of Mary, the true Eve of the human race, that "this is a great mystery—I mean in reference to Christ and to the Church" (Ephesians 5:32, Confraternity text), and, as Saint Jerome said when commenting on this passage, *divinum cor quaerit interpretis*, fully to understand it requires a heart that is divine.[16] We must be spiritual men to comprehend the mystery of Mary in the Church. Thus also Augustine in his *Confessions* explains in terms of the mystery of Mary and the Church the words of the prophet "Return ye to the heart" (Isaiah 46:8), saying:

Christ, our life, came down to us and delivered us from death, killing death itself with the fullness of His life. And now He calls to us with a voice of thunder: return to that hidden sanctuary, whence I came forth to you, return to the primeval and virginal womb, wherein I took human flesh.[17]

It is this return to the heart of Mary that we need today, so that our love of the Church as our Mother may grow together with our love of the Mother of Jesus. Then we can begin to understand once more how the early Christians loved their Mother even to the death, because they loved Mary in the Church, and in both they loved Christ. How profound are the words of a Father of the fourth century:

> Eve looks forward to Mary, and her very name "Mother of all the living" (Genesis 3:20) is a mysterious presage of the future, for Life itself was born of Mary, whence she became more fully "the Mother of all the living"....
>
> Nor can we see the passage "I will put enmities between thee and the woman" (Genesis 3:15) as applying to Eve alone: it received its true fulfilment when that holy and unique One came, born of Mary without work of man....
>
> And then there is that other text nearby "Wherefore a man shall leave father and mother, and shall cleave to his wife, and they shall be two in one flesh" (Genesis 2:24), and this also we can understand of Mary, and, I would even say, of the Church, for the Apostle says of this passage, "This is a great mystery—I mean in reference to Christ and to the Church" (Ephesians 5:32, Confraternity text).
>
> His own Body He fashioned from Mary, and the Church He fashioned from the wound in His own side, when the spear pierced His breast and there flowed out for us the twin redeeming mysteries of the water and the blood.[18]

Chapter Two

Immaculata

From the first instant of Mary's human existence until her Assumption into heaven, every detail of her life that Revelation has provided is a "type of what is to come." The Church is symbolized in Mary.

That is true of the first and underlying mystery of her life, which we know from the sources of Revelation and from the solemn declaration of the Church, namely that Mary in the first instant of her conception, in virtue of the redemptive death to come of her divine son, was preserved free from all stain of original sin. She possessed from the beginning also, precisely as a member of the human race redeemed by Christ, that gift of sanctifying grace which was destined originally for the whole human race from Adam and Eve, and restored to every believer by the death of Christ, the son of Mary. Thus it is that Mary Immaculate is already an essential symbol of the restoration to grace, a work which began on the Cross and will have its entire fulfilment at the end of time by presenting to the eternal Father Adam's family, redeemed into the one glorified Body of Christ: a symbol therefore of the Church. This is how the early Fathers saw in Mary Immaculate the *Ecclesia Immaculata*, and in this figure of the Church Immaculate the glorious conclusion of the work of redemption, which will be revealed on that day when God "who is able to preserve you without sin" will "present you spotless (*immaculatos*) before the presence of His glory with exceeding joy, in the coming of our Lord Jesus Christ" (Epistle of Jude 24).

God's first word of salvation, spoken outside the locked gates of Paradise, already indicates a woman, a single woman, who could never be overcome by Satan: "I will put enmities between thee and the woman, and thy seed and her seed" (Genesis 3:15). This woman was first of all Eve, to whom the astounding promise was made that the Redeemer should come from her race. But the full meaning of the prophecy is only realized when we see foreshadowed in Eve the other "Mother of all the living," who herself should actually give birth to the Savior. "But already then," said Augustine, "Mary was included in Eve; yet it was only when Mary came, that we knew who Eve was."[19] The woman who crushed the serpent's head was the Mother of God-

made-man. From the beginning of Catholic theology
the text has been thus interpreted. Christ, the son of
the woman of the promise, would conquer Satan,
"and therefore God put enmities between the serpent
and the woman, until the promised seed came to crush
its head, the seed of Mary."[20] And again Irenaeus: "He
who should be born of a virgin, He will strike the
serpent's head."[21] And Ephrem the Syrian said in one
of his hymns to our Lady: "The Lord hath spoken it:
Satan is cast out of heaven. And Mary has trodden on
him who struck at the heel of Eve. And blessed be He,
who by His birth has destroyed the foe!"[22]

But this mystery of the Immaculate Conception of
Mary is not only a personal privilege granted to her
who was to become the mother of God. Mary has
thereby become a figure of the Church, for the Church
is the fulfilment of the history that began at Mary's
conception, anticipating the redeeming sacrifice, and
ends with the admission of Adam's race to eternal life,
with the Father, through the Son and in the Holy Spirit.
That is why the Fathers saw in the woman of promise
not only Eve and our Lady, but also the Church, the
mother of the new life, the almighty conqueror of
Satan. Let us listen again to Augustine:

> These words [of Genesis] are a great mystery: here
> is the symbol pointing forward to the Church that
> is to come: she is fashioned out of the side of her
> spouse, out of the side of her spouse in the sleep of
> death. Did not the Apostle say of Adam that he is

"a figure of Him who was to come" (Romans 5:14)?
And is it not also true of the Church? Listen then,
understand and realize: it is she that will tread
down the serpent's head. O Church, watch for the
serpent's head![23]

The Church is therefore the woman, fulfilling
both Eve and Mary, she is at war throughout history,
she has the victory at the end. In the Middle Ages
this was still the interpretation of Genesis: "Enmities
therefore between the serpent and the woman,
between the devil and the Church: for it is the
Church that is foreshadowed by the woman."[24] *Ecclesia
Immaculata*.

There is another place in Scripture where the Fathers
saw a reference to this victory of the Immaculate
Mother, first fulfilled in Mary and then in the
Church's struggles. It is in the longing cry to the bride
in the Canticle (Canticles 5:2): "Open to me, my sister,
my love, my dove, my perfect one." The Latin text, as
used by the Latin Fathers, for the Hebrew "my perfect
one," has *immaculata mea*, a title given in the earliest
times to our Lady. The bride, here greeted by God, is
the mother of God, the "stainless earth" (*terra immaculata*),
a name under which our Lady was invoked in the early
Acts of Andrew the Apostle.[25] For God longed for this
bridal union with humanity in the womb of the spotless
virgin. Ever and again in the early Church's expression of
love of our Lady we find the phrase "Mary Immaculate."[26]
And here are the roots of that dogmatic statement,

which took so long to unfold, namely that Mary who is in every way immaculate, is free from all taint of Adam's hereditary ill. She is the bride, called "immaculate" in the Canticle: "She is immaculate, because she is in every way spiritually and corporally untainted."[27]

In this respect Mary is essentially a symbol of the Church that was to come. Already Origen speaks of the Church as the *immaculata*.[28] And all the interpreters of the Canticle who see the bride as the figure of the Church are constantly making reference to the mystery of the *Ecclesia Immaculata*. The Church is immaculate, because she is cleansed by the waters of baptism, because she is already on the way to the unobstructed vision of God, because she is washed with the blood of Christ, because (in spite of sin and darkness among her children on earth) she stands already glorious without spot or wrinkle before God.[29] "O Church, thou art my sister, my immaculate one, because by me art thou cleansed from all sin."[30] Thus is Mary the type of the Church, since each is a virgin unspotted (*Virgo immaculata*), says Ambrose.[31] All this is of course an echo of the Canticle, but an echo whose sound is strengthened by further words of Scripture, in Saint Paul, who writes of Christ and the Church, that He would "present it to Himself a glorious Church, not having spot or wrinkle, or any such thing, but that it should be holy and without blemish (*sancta et immaculata*)" (Ephesians 5:27). And all the time, up to the Middle Ages, when we find an interpretation of the

Canticle, we always find also the words of Augustine in praise of the *Ecclesia Immaculata*: "Thus saith the Lord: my sister art thou by my blood, my love art thou by my coming, my dove art thou by my spirit, but my perfect one art thou by my word, which them to the full hast received from my mouth."[32]

Ecclesia Immaculata

Exiled humanity, standing at the outer edge of its paradise lost, yet sees in the one figure of Eve and Mary, not only the beginning of the work of God's spirit, but the Church that the figure foreshows, and in this way our own love of the Church together with our own devotion to Mary receives new meaning and new depth from the mystery.

The word "immaculate" indeed sums up the mystery of our own spiritual life. We are members of the Church, and in us the Church's mystery must be accomplished: it begins with Mary Immaculate, and we in our turn, by the power of the Holy Spirit, must once more become immaculate. In each of us the victory over the serpent must be achieved. Each of us must once more find entry to the paradise lost from which Mary was never excluded, entry to the eternal company of God, presented, as Saint Jude says, "spotless before the presence of His glory with exceeding joy." It was Mary's privilege to receive this gift, not returned because never lost, but given in virtue of the redeeming blood of her Son, in order to prepare a place for Him.

And to us, the heirs of Adam, the same gift is returned in virtue of the same blood. Thus Saint Paul never tires of reminding his friends that Christ has "reconciled [you] in the body of His flesh through death, to present you holy and unspotted (*sanctos et immaculatos*) and blameless before Him" (Colossians 1:22), and that God "chose us in Christ before the foundation of the world, that we should be holy and unspotted (*sancti et immaculati*) in His sight" (Ephesians 1:4).

God, in His love and mercy, from all eternity made His choice and looked past all the sins of the world to the death of His beloved son, "who by the Holy Spirit offered Himself unspotted (*immaculatum*) unto God" (Hebrews 9:14). And in this glance from eternity He also saw the one woman, immaculate through the blood of His son, and in her and with her all who belong to her whom we call the Church Immaculate. Hers is the victory over the serpent of error and sin, hers to bring the symbols to fulfilment, the symbols of both Eve and Mary.

Thus it is that the Immaculate Conception of the Mother of God is in the deepest sense the consummation and the reality, the pledge and the beginning of our own personal salvation: "What began in Mary in the flesh, in the spirit is fulfilled in the Church."[33] And here perhaps is another reason why the Church celebrates so near the beginning of her liturgical year the Feast of the Immaculate Conception, for she is celebrating her own mystery, the mystery of our own personal sanctification. "All that we lost through the curse upon Eve is restored to us through the blessing upon Mary... for she is the immaculate one, untouched by sin": the words are those of a Carolingian writer, which we read in the Breviary on December 8 under the name of Saint Jerome.[34] And Saint Bernard's homily (which used to be read on the third day of the octave) speaks of the mystery of Genesis:

> The woman, whom Thou gavest me to be my companion, gave me of the tree, and I did eat. Make haste now, O Eve, and come to Mary; come, O Mother, to thy Daughter! Change those words from a miserable excuse to a song of thanksgiving: Lord, the woman, whom Thou gavest me to be my companion, gave me to eat from the tree of life![35]

The woman is both Mary and the Church, as a thousand years before Saint Bernard Tertullian had already said, speaking of the Church as the new paradise and the woman of the promise: "God knew that it is not good for man to be alone, and He knew how good it would be for him to have a woman with him, first Mary and then the Church."[36]

But the final battle is still to come, for the serpent still lies in wait for the woman's heel. Yet, with Christ, victory is assured, and here is the fulfilment of the revelation of the *Immaculata*, at the frontiers of paradise lost and in the apocalyptic heavens in the mystery of that twelfth chapter:

Look well at the Woman in the Sky, clothed with the sun, crowned with twelve stars, and with the moon spread beneath her feet: yes, it is indeed she, our Mother, it is indeed our Church![37]

Thus one of the great Greek Fathers sings the praises of the Church. And in a quiet cloister of the west we still hear the echo in the ninth century:

We can indeed say that the Woman of Revelation is Mary, because she is the Mother of the Church, having given birth to the Head of the Church. Yet she is also the daughter of the Church, and the holiest of her members.[38]

Chapter Three

Ever Virgin

All the graces given to her who is "full of grace" were given to her with reference to the supreme dignity of being the earthly mother of the Eternal Word. The beginning of this work of grace was her entire freedom from any share in the guilt of original sin, in virtue of the shedding of that blood, for which she as Mother of the Savior was to prepare. But this idea of her divine motherhood is completed by the further grace of her virginal conception of our Lord and her subsequent ever virginal state. Let us now therefore consider this mystery of the faith, this ineffable miracle, in the plan of salvation, in the context of the mystery of the Church. Saint Ambrose calls the Church a virgin,[39] and in the Church the mystery of Mary's perpetual virginity extends to the end of time, when there will begin for the redeemed children of Eve that eternal virginity, of which our Lord spoke when He said that "in the Resurrection they shall neither marry nor be married, but shall be as the angels of God in heaven" (Matthew 22:30).

It is one of the mysteries of our Catholic faith that the Mother of God was a virgin in the conception of her child, and that she remained a virgin after His birth for the rest of her life on earth; and we accept this teaching, as we do that of her own Immaculate Conception, both from Scripture and the Apostolic Tradition.

Moreover, when we enter into the question more deeply, we find that this miracle of the virgin birth is itself proof and evidence of our faith: a "sign," as Isaiah the prophet said: "The Lord Himself shall give you a sign: behold a virgin shall conceive and bear a son" (Isaiah 7:14); for this event, by which God deigned to become man, points the way to that new birth, by which man is "born of the Spirit" (John 3:6), and without which there is no entrance to the Kingdom of Heaven. The virgin birth of the second Adam points to the end of time, when the children of the first Adam, after centuries of birth and death, will be admitted to everlasting life. This is what God promised from the beginning, a paradise of virginal bliss, won for mankind by the virginal birth of the virgin son of man: "The first man was of the earth, earthly, the second man, from heaven, heavenly.... Therefore as we have borne the image of the earthly, let us also bear the image of the heavenly" (1 Corinthians 15:47, 49).

Now in this view of the doctrine of the virgin birth we can see included the whole mystery of the Church. Here also the theology of the Fathers looks from Eve to Mary and through her to the virgin Church. One of their fundamental lines of thought about our Lady, onwards from Justin and Irenaeus, is that already in the creation of Adam from the still virgin earth, the birth of the Word made flesh from the Virgin Mary was foreshadowed, together with the rebirth of mankind from the virgin Church. "Whence came the nature of the first-created man?" asks Irenaeus, and he gives his own reply:

> From God's will and wisdom, and from the virgin earth. And when this man was to be restored to grace, God wished the same path to be followed and to be born in the flesh of the Virgin by God's will and wisdom. And as the first man fell into sin and death through a virgin's disobedience, so mankind was to find life for his soul through a virgin who was obedient to the word of God.[40]

And the Virgin Mary herself became a type of the way that Adam's children were to find their new life: by rebirth from their mother the Church. Thus Irenaeus was able to utter his famous words about our Lady and the Church, seen as one: "How was mankind to escape this birth into death, unless he were born again through faith, by that new birth from the Virgin, the sign of salvation that is God's wonderful and unmistakable gift?"[41] Eve's disobedience was retrieved through Mary's faith, that is the beginning of the Church's faith. Ambrose preached this to his people, and taught them the whole mystery of Adam's rebirth in terms that have become classical:

> See how the selfsame knots that were tied in condemnation are now undone, and how the old footprints are trodden again in the work of salvation: Adam was from the virgin earth, Christ from a virgin; Adam was made in the image of God, Christ is the image of God...; folly came from a woman, wisdom from a virgin; from the tree came death, from the Cross came life.[42]

Let us now look more deeply into the teaching of the Fathers on the Church's virginity, for this idea, so long forgotten but yet so precious, lies at the roots of the mystery of our Lady and the Church.[43] Of course Saint Paul already knew the typological interpretation of Eve, the "mother of all the living," applied to the Church, when he wrote to the Corinthians: "I betrothed you to one spouse, that I might present you a chaste virgin to Christ. But I fear lest, as the serpent seduced Eve by his guile, so your minds may be corrupted, and fall from a single devotion to Christ" (2 Corinthians 11:2-3, Confraternity text). The Church of Corinth is the virgin, and Paul is like the man who gives away the bride. She is forever betrothed to Christ.

But there is always the danger that through Satan's guile she may lose that virginity, through false teaching that may find its way into the community. Here is the center of the teaching later so greatly extended, namely that the virginity of the Church first of all means that she preserves intact her faith in Christ. Heresy means loss of that virginity, it is breaking off the betrothal to Christ.

Thus when the early Christian says that the Church, like Mary, is ever a virgin, and can never fall into Eve's unfaithfulness, he is in fact saying neither more nor less than we say today with our doctrine of the Church's infallibility; for it is undoubtedly true that within the Church as such, Christ's true and unsullied teaching, confided to her care, can never be lost.

It is, however, possible that by the devil's influence error may penetrate into this local Church or that and so rob her of her virginity: that the true and unadulterated teaching of the Apostles may here or there be lost, together with the purity of the faith which Christ brought to the earth, and which had its beginning with Mary's faithful acceptance of her task. This is the meaning of the words, reported of Hegesippus, one of the early Palestinian witnesses (about the year 180), when he says of the Church of Jerusalem that:

> Until now she remained a virgin pure and unspotted, because those who attempted to undermine the sound teaching of the Gospel were kept in obscurity

and out of sight. But when the voices of the holy Apostles had been silenced by their various destinies, and that happy generation had passed away who had with their own ears heard the voice of God's truth itself, then for the first time godless error came in to attack, by means of lying teachers.[44]

Hegesippus is referring to the first great heresy that threatened the Church: that of the Gnostics. The Fathers of the Church, led by Irenaeus, immediately gave battle, to defend the purity of the Apostolic Tradition, which could remain intact only within the virginal bosom of the Church. For she alone is the paradise regained, where Eve can no longer be deceived, where stands the true tree of knowledge and of life. That is the sense of the closing words of the very early Epistle to Diognetus, probably derived from Hippolytus, the disciple of Irenaeus, where the Church's virginity is praised in a kind of rhythmic hymnody. Within that paradise that is the Church, both life and knowledge are but one: in all that is in paradise, God's will alone is done.

> Nought now is there in the serpent's power, no error there nor fraud, no more shall Eve there be deceived, but faith cries out: A Virgin she! Salvation there for all to see, the Apostles are their guides. The Pasch of the Lord is close at hand, the heavenly bodies arrayed in harmony. The Logos speaks to all the saints: through Him be glory to the Father![45]

And a Christian hymn from the early days of the struggle against Gnosticism pictures God's grace as the Church coming down from heaven:

> A Virgin pure she comes,
> And admonishing she cries:
> Ye sons of men, turn back,
> Ye daughters, come back here.
> Leave now those paths of doom,
> And come ye here to me!
> For I will be your guide
> In all the ways of truth,
> That you be not destroyed
> Nor even harmed![46]

A hundred years later, when the storms of error threatened the Church on every side, it was again the great consolation of the Fathers to meditate on the perpetual virginity of the Church. Heresy is unchaste, it is adultery towards Christ.

> The bride of Christ cannot commit adultery, for she is chaste and holy. Everyone who cuts himself off from the Church, and lies with an adulteress, cuts himself off from the Church's promises. He who leaves the Church cannot receive Christ's reward. No one can have God for his father, who has not got the Church for his mother.

These are famous and unforgettable words of Saint Cyprian.[47] After this it was especially Saint Augustine who worked out the idea of the Church's virginity in terms of the mystery of our Lady. This was his sermon one Christmas Day:

> Today the virgin birth is celebrated by the virgin Church. For to her it was that the Apostle said: "I have espoused you to one husband, that I may present you as a chaste virgin to Christ" (2 Corinthians 11:2). Why as a chaste virgin, unless because of her purity in faith, hope and charity? The virginity, which Christ desires in the heart of the Church, He assured first in the body of Mary. But the Church could only be a virgin if she has a spouse, to whom she could give herself entire; and He is a virgin's son.[48]

And as it was Augustine's constant care to protect his people against the errors of Arianism, we find him again emphasizing the picture of the virginal and infallible Church: "Your virginity should be something spiritual. There cannot be many in the Church who are physically virgins, but spiritually every one of the faithful should be a virgin...." The old serpent would indeed destroy them and drive them out of the paradise which is the true Church.... But "watch therefore, watch, O my soul, and guard your own virginity!"[49]

And also the Anglo-Saxon Bede is full of Augustine's theology of the Church and Mary.

> Christ is the true spouse, and the bride is the holy Church. Her children are from every nation, and of her the Apostle spoke when he said: "I have

espoused you to one husband, that I may present you as a chaste virgin to Christ." She is a virgin in the purity of the Spirit, in the perfection of love, in the concord of peace.[50]

Thus the mystery of the perpetual virginity of Mary is continued in the purity of the teaching Church: a chaste womb shelters Christ in His physical and in His mystical body. And rightly the Church praises her in the Breviary (on the feast of her holy name) with the words: "Rejoice, O Virgin Mary: for thou alone hast destroyed all heresies in all the world!"

But there is yet a second way in which the mystery of Mary's perpetual virginity finds its continuation in the mystery of the Church, and it is closely connected with the first. It consists in the special place given to physical virginity throughout the Church's history. This seems to spring from the very nature of the Church and her life of grace, which is always producing new forms of the life of virginity.

Saint Augustine once spoke of the connection between the two ideas: "Christ has made His Church a virgin: she is a virgin in her faith. Physically she has only a small number of consecrated virgins, but according to the faith, all must be virgins, men and women alike."[51]

Therefore just as all Christians, by the power of grace in Baptism, must keep spotless the living treasure of the true faith, so also a few chosen souls will be vowed to keep physical virginity in their bodies: and this is because the Church had her first beginning in the virginal womb of Mary. This is what Leo the Great says: "He came into the world by a new way, for He wished to bring to man's very body a new gift of spotless purity. Man by his birth cannot preserve virginity, but in his rebirth he can set it up as an ideal."[52]

The same Holy Spirit, who overshadowed the Blessed Virgin, is at work in the Sacrament of Baptism (and we shall return to this later), the grace of which gives strength to those who are called to a life of consecrated virginity. Such a life is an image first of the chaste union of the divine and human nature in the womb of the Virgin, and then of the great mystery of the Church. This is the meaning of Ambrose, when he says:

> The Lord appeared in our flesh and in Himself fulfilled the spotless marriage of Godhead and humanity, and since then the eternal virginity of the life of heaven has found its place among men. Christ's mother is a virgin, and likewise is His bride, the Church.[53]

It is therefore directly from the Incarnation and from the grace of Baptism that the holy race descends of which the Pontifical speaks at the consecration of a virgin:

> Alongside of marriage, so solemnly blessed by the Church, there should be a race of still more chosen souls, who, renouncing the bodily union which otherwise befits man and woman, strive after the high mystery which marriage itself indicates, and consecrate that love which marriage symbolizes,

namely to enter the bridal chamber of Him who is both the spouse and the son of eternal virginity.

Here indeed is the great mystery of the Church: the union of the divine and human nature in the womb of the Virgin. Therefore in the same prayer the Church blesses a virgin with the words: "May you be blessed by the creator of heaven and earth, who has deigned to choose you to share the life of the Blessed Mary, the Mother of our Lord Jesus Christ." Her life is to be the example. "Your example is now the life of Mary, from which shines forth as from a mirror all the beauty of chastity and the pattern of every virtue": these are the words of Ambrose to the consecrated virgins of the early Church.[54] If the Church is to remain faithful to her vocation—"a virgin she is, and so may she ever be!" said Augustine,[55]—there must always be these "chosen souls" who follow Mary in what she was, and show the way to what the blessed will be in heaven.

But the life of heaven is in the future: the present is amid the darkness of error and sin. Only in the everlasting glory of Christ will the Church's mission become plain: her labors to protect the faith unsullied and chastity in all its beauty; since for this the Son of God was born man of a virgin. Eve is turned forever into Mary, and the joy of joys will be realized: the children of Eve become the children of the virgin Church, forever possessing by her the truth of Christ, in her sanctified and purified for the day when the Lord comes.

Every time we proclaim our belief in the Church, we are paying honor to Mary, and every witness of our love for Mary is a witness of our belief in the Church: for in Mary the Church became the Virgin Mother of God. Let us therefore hasten to meet that day, when Jesus will appear in all His glory, and let us cry with Augustine:

> *Speciosus forma prae filiis hominum*: "beautiful above the sons of men" (Psalm 44:3), Mary's Son, spouse of the Church! He has made His Church like to His mother, He has given her to us as a mother, He has kept her for Himself as a virgin. The Church, like Mary, is a virgin ever spotless and a mother ever fruitful.
>
> What He bestowed on Mary in the flesh, He has bestowed on the Church in the spirit: Mary gave birth to the One, and the Church gives birth to the many, who through the One become one.[56]

Chapter Four

Mother of God

The words of Augustine with which we concluded our meditation on the Church's everlasting virginity indicate the very center of the mystery of Mary and the Church: "Mary gave birth to the One, and the Church gives birth to the many, who through the One become one." For the ineffable and unique grace given to the Virgin Mary, to become the mother of the everlasting Word, is the immediate source of all the other graces which the heavenly Father gave to her, that she might provide "a worthy habitation for His son," as we say in the collect for the Immaculate Conception.

In this sense precisely Mary is the great symbol of the Church: for in the teaching of the Fathers we find that not only is the virgin Church truly a mother because she has given birth to us, the many, into everlasting life, but also because she is "the Mother of God" in that she is ever giving new life to the Mystical Body of Christ. In the mystery she is the mother of the one and the whole Christ.

Here we reach one of the profoundest elements in the Mariology of the Fathers, and it is important to study it carefully, so that neither our faith nor our piety be led astray in the inquiry. Yet we Christians of today can be as fearless as the great theologians of earlier centuries, especially as we have before us the directions of our Holy Father Pius XII in his encyclical *Mystici Corporis*, of which one particular passage gives us courage indeed: "We would in no way reproach those who are seeking ways and means to penetrate the supreme mystery of our incorporation in Christ, and according to their ability to clarify its meaning."[57]

This is then our intention: to consider that profound but almost forgotten area of Patristic teaching which is the Marian mystery of the Church, and to find out what the early Christians meant when joyfully they sang the praises of the Church as the "holy Mother of Christ."

The starting point is the fundamental mystery of Mary's life, that she was overshadowed by the Holy Spirit, to become in a true and exact sense the "Mother of God." Every believing Christian knows how to understand this: Mary is the human mother in whose womb that human nature was formed, which from the first moment of its existence was united to the second person of the Godhead, the everlasting Word. That "which shall be born of thee shall be called the Son of God" (Luke 1:35). If Mary therefore from the earliest times was called the "Mother of God," this was simply a proclamation of the fundamental belief in the one and only Lord Jesus Christ, in whom the divine and the human are indivisible, unmixed and inseparable. And when in the fifth century, under the influence of the speculations of the later Greeks, the title came to be denied her, the faithful conscience of the whole Church of the East rose up, and at the General Council of Ephesus in 431 the truth of Mary's dignity as Mother of God was solemnly proclaimed. In every *Ave Maria* we greet our Lady as "Mother of God," and when in 1931 the Church celebrated the fifteenth centenary of Ephesus, Pope Pius XI wrote an encyclical to mark the occasion and said:

> If the son of the Blessed Virgin Mary is true God, then it is meet and just that the woman who gave birth to Him should be called the "Mother of God." And further, if Jesus is a single person, and moreover a divine person, then Mary should most certainly be called the Mother, not only of Christ the Man, but of God—the *Theotokos*. She was already greeted by her cousin Elizabeth as "the Mother of my Lord" (Luke 1:43), Ignatius the Martyr said that she had given birth to God, and in his turn Tertullian proclaimed that God was born of Mary.[58]

That is the faith of the Church from the beginning until now.

Let us try therefore to arrive at a deeper understanding of the symbolic content of this truth of our faith with reference to the Church, for we find ourselves here confronted with the very roots of the doctrine which we call the "Mystical Body of Christ." Now Saint Paul says of Christ that "He is the head of the body, the Church" (Colossians 1:18), and all members of the human family that is the offspring of Adam, who are born again of water and the Holy Spirit form the One Mystical Body of Christ, as again Saint Paul says: "We being many, are one body in Christ" (Romans 12:5). The exact way in which this mysterious unity is achieved must of course remain a mystery in the obscurity of faith while we are still here below, and moreover, as Pope Pius XII has warned us, we must guard against any sort of identification of Christ and the Christians which would as it were remove from individual Christians their physical and moral independence. On the other hand we shall take care not to empty the doctrine of its meaning, but on the contrary to preserve the teaching of the Apostles and the early Church, where this unity of the faithful in Christ is always insisted upon.

This unity with Christ [says Pope Pius XII] is represented as so essential, that according to the words of the Apostle (Colossians 1:18) it can be regarded as the central teaching, continually uttered by the

Fathers, that the Divine Savior, together with His Body made up of many, constitutes a single mystical person, or, as Augustine puts it, "the whole Christ."[59]

We can therefore speak of the Church in this precise sense as the whole Body of Christ, or the "Mystical Christ."

It is now our task to fit into the framework of this doctrine all that the theology of the early Church has to say of the symbolic relationship of Mary as the Mother of God, and the Church. The *Mater Ecclesia* is truly the Mother of God on earth, since in virtue of the sacramental power derived from Christ she brings to birth into everlasting life the members of His Body, that is, the "whole Christ." This becomes clearer if we begin by detaching the idea of the Church as the "Mother of Christ," leaving aside for the moment the complementary idea of the Church as the lifegiving Mother of each of the faithful. The doctrine of the Mystical Body was so vividly present to the Fathers of the early Church, that they had no hesitation in thinking of the Church as the Mystical Mother of God, as the virgin who bears the Logos in her heart, as the fulfilment of Mary the Virgin and Mother.

Let us begin our study of this "Mariology of the Church" with the Roman theologian Hippolytus, who was heir through Irenaeus and the theology of Asia Minor to John and the Book of Revelation. The great picture of the woman in the twelfth chapter (of which we shall speak more particularly later) is indeed a picture of the Church and her history, but applicable also to the Virgin Mary. When Hippolytus is explaining this chapter of Revelation, he says:

> The Church never ceases to give birth to the Logos. "And she brought forth a man-child who was to rule all nations" says the text: the perfect man that is Christ, the child of God, both God and man. And the Church brings forth this Christ when she teaches all nations.[60]

The Church, then, is the mother of the Word; and it is not mere chance that Hippolytus was the first to call the Virgin Mary the "Mother of God" and the "mother of the Word."

The other great theologian of the third century, Origen, who in his youth once went from Alexandria to Rome in order to hear the word of God from Hippolytus, himself developed the same idea into a remarkable mystical interpretation of the Nativity and Christmas.[61] Unceasingly, he says in a sermon, the Church renews in herself the mystery of that night, when the angels came down to announce the birth of God from Mary: "Hear this, O shepherds of the churches, O shepherds of God: all through time the angel comes down and announces to you that today and every day the Redeemer is born, that is Christ the Lord."[62] This mystery, he says, is realized "in the innermost heart" of the *Ecclesia Immaculata*.[63] As Mary once conceived the Logos through the "word of faith," so now the Church, like Mary, gives birth to the Word, the Logos carried in her heart. What happened with Mary through the overshadowing of the Holy Spirit, is daily renewed mystically within the Church. And at the end of the period of persecution we find similar ideas in Methodius, the martyr of Philippi, who greatly developed the theology of Origen:

> It would be wrong to proclaim the Incarnation of the Son of God from the holy Virgin, without admitting also His Incarnation in the Church. Every one of us must therefore recognize His coming in the flesh, by the pure Virgin, but at the same time recognize His coming in the spirit of each one of us.[64]

And again Methodius speaks of the woman of Revelation in his *Symposium of the Ten Virgins*: "The woman who brings forth the man-child that is the Logos in the hearts of the faithful is our mother the Church."[65] And again: "Therefore the Church is in labor and travail, until Christ is formed and born within us, so that every one of the saints, insofar as he shares in Christ, is Christ born again."[66]

The Church of the East has never forgotten this, and even in a fourth-century document of church law we find these phrases:

> The Church is the daughter of the Most High, and she lies in travail on your account, for she, through

the word of grace, forms Christ within you. For by sharing in Him you become His holy and chosen members, and in faith by baptism you are made perfect, to the image of Him who created you.[67]

And in the seventh century the monk Anastasius of Sinai expresses in a hymn of praise his belief in the Marian dignity of the Church, when he addresses the Church in these words: "O blessed art thou among women, holy Church, source of life, lifegiving mother of the faithful, glorious mother of Christ!" And why is the Church truly the mother of the Lord? "Because blessed is the fruit of thy womb, the one people from all living nations!"[68]

When we turn to the Latin West, it is of course Saint Augustine who is the great interpreter of the mystery of Mary and the Church. Admittedly he speaks chiefly of the Church's motherhood towards the faithful, but there are clear indications in his sermons of his deep penetration of the theological problem of the mystical unity which binds together the multitudes of Christians in the unity of Christ. He often asks how and in what way we can say of the Church that she is truly the "Mother of Christ." On one occasion he invites his hearers to ponder the question:

> The Church is a virgin. Perhaps you will say: If she is a virgin, how can she beget children? Or, if she does not bear children, how can we claim to be born from her womb? My answer is: She is both

virgin and mother; she is like Mary who gave birth
to the Lord. Was not Mary a virgin when she gave
birth, and did she not remain ever a virgin; But the
Church also gives birth and yet remains a virgin.
And when you consider it more closely, she gives
birth to Christ Himself, for all who receive baptism
are His members. Does not the Apostle say: "You
are the body of Christ, member for member" (1
Corinthians 12:27, Confraternity text)? If then she
gives birth to Christ's members, she is in every way
like to Mary.[69]

On another occasion he explained the same idea to his
people in lively terms:

Mark well, O my friends, how the Church is the
bride of Christ. That is indeed well known, but
what is much more difficult to see, yet none the
less true, is that the Church is Christ's Mother.
Mary the Virgin, the symbol of her, went before
her; and how, I ask you, is Mary Christ's Mother, if
not because she gave birth to His members? And
you, to whom I am speaking now, are Christ's
members: and who gave birth to you? I can already
hear the answer that comes from your hearts: our
mother the Church. She is then the holy and
glorious mother, who is like to Mary, who is both
virgin and mother, who gives birth to Christ—and
you are Christ's members.[70]

Many more examples from the rich spiritual treasury
of Augustine could be quoted, to show how brilliantly

that great man expounds the mystery of the "Church as Mother of God," but indeed wherever he speaks of Mary and the Church, he sounds the depths of that mystery: "She is most truly our mother, because the Church every day in baptism brings new Christians to birth, who simply because they are Christians form the one and only Christ."[71]

And the spiritual sons of Augustine, during the slow development of the German Middle Ages, continued faithfully to proclaim the same doctrine. "Let the Church of Christ rejoice," says an anonymous preacher of the sixth century, "for on the pattern of the Blessed Mary she also has become the mother of a divine child."[72] And it was Gennadius of Marseilles who expressed it in one sentence which the whole Middle Ages thought was Augustine's: "The Church is ever in travail to bring forth the one Christ in His members."[73] And Berengaud in the Carolingian age said: "The Church every day gives birth to the members of Him, whom Mary the Virgin once brought to birth: for Christ and His members are but one single Christ."[74] And finally Haymo of Halberstadt in the ninth century:

> Mary is also a member of the Church; yet since she is the blessed Mother of God, she herself represents the Church. For in her, that is to say in the Church, the sign is every day fulfilled, since in the Church every day Christ is conceived and brought to birth.[75]

Still later, Albert the Great, the master of Aquinas, tells us: "Every day the Church gives birth to Christ Himself, through faith in the hearts of those who listen."[76]

There it is, drawn with a few strokes, the picture of high mystery of the Church as the Fathers saw it. She is the Mother of God. The Church marches through the dark centuries, as Mary marched through the dark countryside from Nazareth to Bethlehem, with the word of God in her heart. "*Quotidie*," said Augustine so often, and his word was so gladly taken up by the Middle Ages—"every day" this mystery of the birth of God is fulfilled in the Church. In one of his most beautiful passages the Anglo-Saxon Bede describes Mary's journey from Nazareth (meaning the "Flower") to Bethlehem (the "House of Bread"), as the journey of the Church, God's Mother:

> Today and every day to the end of time the Lord is unceasingly conceived at "Nazareth" and born at "Bethlehem," whenever one of the faithful takes to himself the "Flower" of the word, he is transformed into an everlasting "House of Bread." Every day the Lord is conceived in a virginal womb, that is, in the spirit of the faithful, and brought to birth in baptism. Every day the Church as God's Mother follows her Master from Galilee (which means the "turning wheel" of life on earth) to that city in Judea (which means the city of "exaltation and praise"), in order to be inscribed in the register of

her dedication to the eternal king. Thus does the Church follow the blessed and ever-virgin Mary, who is the symbol of her, at once espoused and undefiled. She conceives us by the Holy Spirit, and as a virgin brings us to birth without travail.[77]

For we are indeed Christ Himself.

When we come to consider these fundamental ideas of the Fathers about Mary and Church in relation to our own spiritual lives, we at once notice that we are growing to a deeper understanding of the power of the sacraments, which in the womb of the Church are building us up to a Christlike way of life. It is within the Church that this everlasting birth is realized. Eternal life means union with Christ, and this union is already experienced in a mystical and sacramental way within the Church. It is in the sacraments therefore, and first of all in baptism and the Eucharist, that Christ Himself is conceived, born and formed within us. Thus one of the great theologians of today, Matthias Scheeben in his *Mysterien des Christentums*, can write of this mystery of the Church that is both sacramental and Marian:

> The Church's priesthood should bring Christ Himself again to birth in the womb of the Church, in the Eucharist and in the hearts of the faithful, through the power of Christ's spirit at work in the Church. Thus is His Mystical Body actually built up, just as Mary by the power of the same spirit

gave birth to the Word made flesh and gave Him His true Body. Christ's conception and birth in the womb of the Virgin is at once the symbol and the reason for the new conception and birth of Christ in the Church.[78]

With this attitude we are indeed far from feeling any conflict between our love of our mother the Church and our devotion to our mother Mary. Whoever loves the Church, loves the mystery of the divine motherhood, and whoever has a childlike devotion to Mary, has found the entrance to the deepest mystery of the Church.

One of the great writers of the early Church, Clement of Alexandria, saw the majestic figure of the Church in the figure of the Virgin Mother of God. And with him we Christians of today can pay our honor to the beloved and holy mother of God, the Church, the mother of everlasting life which is Christ Himself:

> There is one who is called both a mother and virgin,
> And my joy is to call her by her name of the Church.
> Christ's Body she nurtures by the power of the Word,
> The people reborn, for whom the Lord on the Cross
> Hung in agony, lovingly cradling as children
> And wrapping them deep in the blood of His Godhead.[79]

Chapter Five

Mother of the Faithful

The mystery of the mystical motherhood of the Church, which we have been studying, has another aspect, which we must now look at more closely. Mary, through her position as the mother of God, stands indeed in a special relationship to all mankind who have been formed into a single body through the power of the redeeming blood of her son: Mary is truly the mother of all the redeemed. And it is for us here to observe how the various details of her life as told in the Gospel combine to show her as the symbol of the *Mater Ecclesia*. We have already heard Augustine say: "Our mother the Church is the holy and glorious mother, who is like to

Mary, who is both virgin and mother, who gives birth to Christ—and you are Christ's members."[80]

Let us try then to reach a deeper understanding of Mary's position as mother of God, which means that Mary is the mother of our Lord and that the Church is the mother of all the faithful. These notions once more go back to foundations of the theology of the Church among the early Christians. First of all, Mary is simply the great symbol of the Church. Then, in the notion of her motherhood of all the redeemed we can see developing the notion of that power of transforming the world, according to which the Church as a mother receives into her womb the thousands of generations of the pagan world and invests them with new life in Christ. It was Isidore of Seville who collected in his book *The Allegories* the symbolic interpretations given by the Fathers of the various persons in the Bible, and he says: "Mary stands for the Church. For the Church is espoused to Christ, and as a virgin conceives us, and brings us to birth as a virgin."[81] And in the liturgy of Milan there is that wonderful preface for the dedication of a church—a text that comes from the fifth century—where the Church is spoken of as "mother of all the living, blessed woman with a multitude of children. Every day she bears children to God by the Holy Spirit."[82]

The ideas of Mary and the Church in early Christian theology stand out most plainly in the interpretation in a typological sense of the passages where Mary appears simply as *Mulier*, the "woman," in the story of the Gospel, particularly in three places: the conception and birth of her Son, at the marriage-feast at Cana, and at the death of Christ on the Cross.

The beginning of our Redemption lies in the ineffable decree of the eternal Father to send His only Son, made man. In this divine decree was included the free decision of a human person, in virtue of a special grace, to accept the task of becoming the Mother of the Son of man. And in this free consent of the Virgin Mary is included all that was to follow in God's bestowal of grace on the race of Adam. Her word was in a true sense the beginning of the Church. Augustine put it in a famous phrase: "Mary is indeed the mother of Christ's members, that is, of ourselves. For it is by her work of love that men have been born in the Church, faithful men who are the body of the head, whose mother she was in the flesh."[83]

This "work of love" is first of all her response to the angel, the word that opened the floodgates of God's grace upon mankind, when the Word was made flesh. The Church thus truly began her existence, as the Fathers so often said, in the womb of the Virgin Mary. The union of Godhead and manhood in the one person is the beginning of the fulfilment of the decree of the Father that transformed the world, and all that follows, from the redeeming death of Mary's child upon the Cross to His final glorious return, in other words the whole history of the Church, is no more than an unfolding of the one mystery which began in the heart of Mary. It is the unique mystery of the Church, which is celebrated in a wonderful hymn of the eighth century:

> Sing we the Church's mystery with a hymn to Christ, the Word of the Father, born of a woman, His mother. Great is the mystery entrusted to Mary.[84]

The "great mystery" of which Saint Paul speaks with reference to the Church, has its beginning in the womb of Mary. This is what Paulinus of Nola also meant, when he sang in a wedding-song of the mystery of the union of the Word with human nature in the Virgin's womb: for it is, he said, "a mystical picture of the marriage of Christ and the Church," since it is in the innermost nature of the Church to be the mother of all the redeemed, and so to present in herself the mystery of the Incarnation: "As mother she receives the seed of the eternal Word: she carries nations in her womb, and nations she brings forth to the light."[85]

And Pope Saint Leo, in the classical language of his theology, speaks in one of his Christmas sermons about this mystery of the Church:

> Whenever we adore the Incarnation of our Redeemer, we are thereby celebrating the beginning of our own new life. When Christ was begotten, Christianity began. The birthday of the head is the birthday also of the body.
>
> However divided we may be through various tasks, however scattered through the ages

of time, all of us as children of the Church, the mass of us rising from the river of baptism, have all been born with Christ at His birth.[86]

Christmas for the early Church was a feast of the Church; Mary contains in herself all the mysteries fulfilled in ourselves at our rebirth. But we will speak again of the mystery of baptism when we speak of "Mary at the font."

In the birth of our Lord from Mary the theology of the Fathers sees the great return of all nations, born again from the womb of the virgin Church. Thus in the ancient Preface of the Gelasian Sacramentary we find the words: "Great is the Church's gladness, when she sees her children's birth."[87] Of all the words of the mysticism of the early Church, perhaps none gathers together these thoughts better than those of the sermon on our Lady by Ildephonsus of Toledo:

> There is the Virgin Mary, in whose womb is signified as by a pledge or earnest the whole Church; and we believe most firmly that thus the Church remains securely and forever united to God.[88]

It was this mystery of the union of Godhead and manhood at the heart of the Mother of God that provided the fullness of the medieval love of our Lady: this was the basis of the thought of the early Church, developed into its application to the Church, and then turned back to the devotion to Mary. Of particular

importance to our study therefore is a passage from a
medieval commentary on the Canticle:

> The pious reader may apply this exposition of the
> Canticle to our Lady Saint Mary, not thereby
> contradicting the Fathers of former days who rather
> interpreted the Song with regard to love for the
> Church, but on the contrary completing their
> interpretation, since the present exposition gathers
> together the loving voices of the great worldwide
> Body of Christ, and unites them in the single and
> unique soul of Mary, beloved of Christ above all.
> For there is nothing that cannot be applied to her,
> which has been said or can be said of the Church
> and the great and holy love of her, so beloved of
> Christ, and He so beloved of her.[89]

The mystery of Mary's motherhood towards all the
faithful can be seen in the details of her life, which,
however, the Gospel records with a truly holy brevity,
since we are only told those things which are directly
concerned with the Messianic mission and Mary's part
in the divine plan.

The mystery of the marriage of the divine and the
human at the Incarnation, with which our Redemption
began, appears again at the beginning of our Lord's
ministry, on the occasion of the first miracle worked to
bear witness to His divinity. This was at the marriage-
feast at Cana. Now Saint John, the evangelist with the
deepest feeling for Messianic typology, is not going
merely to report the fact of what happened at a quiet

country wedding; for him the occurrence is but the veil that hides the high mysteries of salvation. The facts that He worked the miracle of changing water into wine at Mary's request, and that He then made an allusion to His "hour" that was not yet come, these things give us a glimpse of the revelation itself. Our Lord calls her "woman," using the word that takes us back at once to the beginning of revelation at the gates of paradise lost; and He uses the same title, when His "hour" was come, and He fulfilled His redeeming agony on the Cross, while she stood by as the great mother of all the faithful. After this she is always "the woman," the true "mother of all the living," the new Eve, the mother of the Body of Christ, who through her had the victory over evil.

When we read in the story of the marriage at Cana the simple words "and the mother of Jesus was there" (John 2:2) we are already deep in symbolism. It was a marriage, and the God-man changed the water of human nature into the wine of the divine; at the feast of Jesus through all time, that is in the Church, the mother of Jesus is there. The history of the Incarnation begins in her; at her motherly request the guests at table become His guests, receiving what He had to give them. The Syrian Ephrem in one of his hymns on the mysteries of the Lord exclaims:

Cana is the praise of Thee, for through Thee came the joy of this feast. The bride is Thy holy Church, the guests at table are Thy guests, and the triumph of the miracle looks forward to Thy coming in majesty.[90]

This deep significance of the marriage at Cana therefore includes the whole history of salvation from the first coming at the Incarnation to our Lord's return at the end of days. Throughout this history, extending through the centuries, humanity is being changed into the wine of the life of grace, while Mary is there, the mother who cares and who intercedes, standing at the very center of the mystery in which God takes human nature from the child of Eve: Mary is mother of all who are sanctified by their faith in this coming of God.

The Benedictine Rupert of Deutz in the early Middle Ages has summed up for us all the ideas of the profoundly symbolic thought of the Fathers about Cana:

And there was a marriage in Cana of Galilee. The whole household is rejoicing, and the household is the Church. "And the mother of Jesus was there," when this marriage was celebrated, for not one of the children or guests at this marriage is ignorant of how Christ became man. No false teachers are children of this marriage: they have their feasts elsewhere, where the mother of Jesus is not. Whatever errors they teach, they all agree in one thing: they have driven out from their hearts and from their conventicles the true faith about the Incarnation. And the only true festival and heavenly marriage-feast is the one where the mother of Jesus

is there—and that means the Church, the mother,
is there. And here every day by the espousals of
virginal souls to Christ is the true faith in God
made man proclaimed.[91]

Here once again it becomes plain that there is a
common ground for the fact that all heresies are
ultimately a denial of the Incarnation of our Lord,
beginning with a refusal to honor His holy mother
and continuing with a rejection of the virginity of the
Church: where the mother of Jesus is not, there can be
no marriage. For she is the woman, who alone has
overcome all heresies, because as virgin and mother she
is the symbol of the Church, which will always hold
fast to the fullness of Christ's revelation and thus
preserve ever unspotted her virginity; and this she will
achieve precisely through bringing to birth the
multitude of nations which she carries in her womb.
Mary is ever present, and ever voicing the needs of the
nations: "They have no wine." The marriage-feast
continues among the nations begotten of Eve. For the
Church is ever present, the mother of all the living, the
mother of Jesus.

So we reach the central point of the work of
redemption. Already the Incarnation itself has pointed
the way, for birth is but the prelude to death. And
Jesus at Cana spoke of His "hour" that was to come:
the hour of His death on the cross, when His blood,
prepared by Mary, was poured out for man's salvation,
for the changing of mankind into God's wine. Again

Jesus speaks solemnly to "the woman" of the world's history: she is to be the mother of the faithful and so also the symbol of the Church. "Woman, behold thy son." And then to John the Apostle: "Behold thy mother" (John 19:26, 27). Here again is the veil: behind the visible anxiety of Jesus about His mother lies hidden the mystery of the Church, which John would have us understand. John stands for the whole of mankind, the Church of those who have been called. To the Church Mary is given as a mother, the Church is entrusted as a mystical child to "the woman." And this interpretation according to the spiritual sense has always been the interpretation of the words of the dying Savior.

It is necessary, in order to understand the depths of such mysteries, to have, as Jerome once said, a "godly" heart. And Origen similarly, in his introduction to Saint John's Gospel, says that none can penetrate this mystery save one who "himself has rested on the breast of Jesus and from Jesus has taken Mary as his mother to his own." And he continues:

> None is Mary's son but Jesus alone; and when therefore Jesus says to His mother, "Behold thy son," it is as if He said "Behold this man is Jesus Himself, to whom thou gavest birth." For everyone who has received the fullness that is baptism, lives now no more himself, but Christ lives in him. And since Christ lives in him, the word to Mary applies to him: "Behold thy son—the anointed Christ."[92]

Thus the mystery of baptism becomes clearer through this last will and testament on the cross: Christ has brought all mankind into one, and has solemnly given her as a mother, for she contains within herself the very symbol of the union between God and man, a union consummated on the cross. Henceforth she is simply the mother of the Church. Thus Ephrem Syrus said in a few words: "Christ gave to John Mary as his Church."[93] And Ambrose similarly says quite briefly, that in this word of the dying Lord is fulfilled the "mystery of the Church."[94] And elsewhere he develops the idea still further, when he tells his people to become like the Apostle John, the "son of thunder" (Mark 3:17):

> Be also yourselves "sons of thunder." You ask me, How can I become a "son of thunder"? You can indeed, if you rest not upon the ground, but upon the breast of Christ. You will become a "son of thunder," if you are a son of the Church. Christ on the cross will call to you, "Behold thy son": then you will begin to be a son of the Church, if you look at Christ conquering on the cross.[95]

It is becoming plainer: Mary and the Church are one; the woman at the foot of the cross is the woman of the promise that would overcome Satan. On the cross we see the fulfilment of what was announced at the gates of paradise lost: that the seed of the woman should crush the serpent's head. The Church is the

great mother of the sons of thunder, who with Christ
bear away the victory. And this is the significance in
the ivory carvings of the Carolingian period of the
second figure beside our Lady beneath the cross, and
opposite to John: this is the figure of the Church, and
shows that this is the instant of the Church's fulfilment.[96] Beneath the victorious cross of the dying God
stands the woman who has won all God's battles, the
holy *Ecclesia*, the fulfilment of Mary. And when the holy
seer, Hildegarde of Bingen, had a vision of the woman
standing beneath the cross, she also heard a voice:
"And I heard, and a voice from heaven spoke: 'She
shall be Thy bride, My son, for the Redemption of My
people: she shall be the people's mother, giving birth
again to the souls saved by the Spirit and by water.'"[97]

And again, Gerhoh of Reichersberg meditated deeply on this mystery:

Next to her son, Mary is the beginning of the holy
Church. For she is the mother of the Apostle, to
whom it was said: "Behold thy mother."

But what is said to one, can be understood as
spoken to all the Apostles, those Fathers of the new
Church. And moreover because Christ had prayed
for all those who should receive the faith through
those same Apostles, that they should all be one, so
the same words can be understood of all the
faithful, who love Christ with all their hearts. What
was said to the one, to John who so loved Him and
whom Christ loved more than all the others, can
be applied to all who love Him.[98]

And at a later date Pope Leo XIII summed up this Patristic interpretation of the motherhood of Mary and of the Church, the mystery which the crucified Savior left as His loving testament:

> It has always been the Church's interpretation that Christ indicated in the person of John the human race, and in particular those who would be faithful to Him. And most truly is Mary the Church's mother, and guide, and the queen of the Apostles.[99]

Thus we can distinguish a Messianic pattern that forms a single shining path of revelation through the sacred books: first there is the revelation of the woman and the victory to come (Genesis 3:15), and then the woman of the mystical marriage of Cana (John 2:4), and finally the woman beneath the cross (John 19:27). Eve received her fulfilment in Mary, but both are symbols of the great mother of all peoples born of Christ, of the *Mater Ecclesia*.

How lovable she is, this mother of ours! Let us offer thanks to the Father and to Christ our brother, that we have been granted to be children of Mary our mother, of our mother the Church. And let us say it once more: there can be no contradiction between a tender devotion to Mary and a deep love of the Church. We can always be ready to exclaim with Ambrose, in a transport of delight about belonging to the Church:

> Where is there a woman like to the Church in multitude of children? A virgin in her mysteries, a

mother of the nations, so fruitful is she that the Scripture says of her: "Many are the children of the desolate, more than of her that hath a husband" (Isaiah 53:1). The Church stands untouched by evil, and fruitful by the Spirit.[100]

In her motherhood of all the faithful she fulfills the deepest mystery of Mary and the Church. The heavenly words spoken to the Virgin Mother of God, when God had become man within her, are spoken for all time to the Virgin Mother the Church: "Blessed art thou among women." And still today we Christians echo the same words, together with that silent monk in the seventh century upon Mount Sinai:

Once again I cry out those words: "Blessed art thou among women," for thou alone, O holy Church, art so blessed: thou with thy bridal garland, thou with the blessing of children, thou, O shining bright Church of God and of Christ! Thou alone art blessed among women, thou and no other![101]

Chapter Six

Mary at the Font

I t may be that the foregoing discussions
of the mystery that unites Mary and the
Church have seemed somewhat difficult
and unfamiliar to the devout reader of today. Yet in
the present age of so little faith it is important to put
ourselves once more in touch with the thought of the
early Church, and to rediscover the treasures laid up in
the writings of the Fathers. And this inevitably means
hard work. But the reader who has been able to view
the mystery of the Church from this Marian aspect,
will surely have noticed the value of these lines of
thought for the development of his own spiritual life.

The next considerations will therefore be concerned
with the application of these dogmatic studies of the

Church as the immaculate Mother of Christ and of the faithful to our own personal sanctification.

The life of the spirit, that supernatural life springing from the gift of grace given to us by Christ, had its beginning for each one of us in the sacrament of baptism. It was then that our holy Mother the Church, by the power of the Holy Spirit, brought us to a new birth in Christ. And it is this rebirth of our whole selves in baptism that is the beginning of the gradual growth in grace during our life on earth which has its fulfilment in the blessed vision of God, when we are to "be made partakers of the divine nature" (2 Peter 1:4) in heaven.

Scripture itself has no better word than "birth," or more precisely "rebirth," since this raising up of our fallen nature, laid low by original sin, builds up our very being and all of which we are capable, into a "new man" (Ephesians 4:24, Colossians 3:10). And it was Christ's word in one of His basic statements about the kingdom of God: "Unless a man be born again of water and the Holy Spirit, he cannot enter into the kingdom of God" (John 3:5). And Saint Paul speaks of baptism as "the laver of regeneration, and renovation of the Holy Spirit" (Titus 3:5).

These things we are all aware of. But we may derive spiritual profit from considering this same mystery in the spirit of the early Church, by linking the idea of baptismal rebirth with the birth of God from the Blessed Virgin. Saint Paul already does this when he says to Titus (3:3-5): "When the goodness and kindness of God our Savior appeared... He saved us by the laver of regeneration." And similarly Saint John links closely together the phrase "The Word was made flesh" and the idea of our spiritual rebirth in the phrase "As many as received Him, He gave them power to be made the sons of God... born not of blood, nor of the will of the flesh, nor of the will of man, but of God" (John 1:12-14).

Our rebirth in baptism is therefore symbolized in the birth which, overshadowed by the Spirit, gave us the Redeemer born of the Virgin. If then the Church as the Mystical Body of Christ is ever being born again in the sacrament of baptism, if "in one Spirit we are all baptized into one body... and in one Spirit we have all been made to drink" (1 Corinthians 12:13), then baptism is forever a continuation of the birth of God made man, born of the Virgin, conceived by the Spirit. This is the old theology of baptism, which will perhaps enable us to understand more deeply the beginning of grace in our own souls, with the attendant figures of the mother of Jesus and our mother the Church. We have therefore called this chapter "Mary at the Font."

Let us first recall a text of Irenaeus, which we have mentioned before: "How was mankind to escape this birth into death, unless he were born again through faith, by that new birth from the Virgin, the sign of salvation that is God's wonderful and unmistakable gift?"[102] These words, from a theologian who was the heir of Saint John, of course apply first to the Virgin

Mary, but insofar as she is a type of the Church, the mother of the Mystical Body, they also apply to the birth of the children of salvation in baptism.

Mary is therefore in a real sense the beginning of our baptismal grace, so that Irenaeus, a little farther on, can state it simply: "Chastely Christ opened the chaste womb, so that thence men also might similarly be reborn."[103] And it is not a different idea, but a continuation of the same symbolic relationship of Mary to the Church, when Ambrose says: "Christ alone opened the silent, immaculate and fruitful womb of the holy Church for the birth of the people of God."[104] The beginning is with Mary: the fulfilment is with baptism, which draws forth the Body of Christ from the womb of the virgin mother, which is the Church.

Ephrem the Syrian has a lovely song about this rebirth of mankind through baptism, beginning with the birth of the child from the Virgin Mary:

> Thy divine birth, O Lord, gave birth to all creatures;
> Born again, mankind was born of her
>   who gave birth to Thee.
> Mankind gave birth to Thee in the body:
>   in the spirit Thou gavest birth to mankind.
> The beginning of Thy coming was Thy birth:
>   to give birth to men was its conclusion;
> Thy birth gave birth to all.
> Praise to Thee, who becamest a child,
>   to make all things new.[105]

Thus Christmas becomes a feast of baptism, and Augustine also said the same thing in his own way:

> God was born of man, so that man could be born again of God. He needed a mother on earth, a Father He had in heaven. He, through whom all things were made, was born of God from all eternity: but He was born of a woman, that He might make all things new.[106]

Here, as with Ephrem, is Mary the mother of God standing as representative, as symbol of mankind, the womb from which God came forth, in order thence to bring mankind to birth anew.

The womb of Mary is the womb of the Church. Still to be seen in that ancient prototype of all baptisteries at the Lateran is the inscription carved in the marble, which proclaims in the poetry of the fifth century the Marian mystery of the Church's motherhood through baptism:

> The Church, Virgin-Mother, brings forth from the River
> The children she conceived by the breath of God.[107]

The author of these lines was none less than Leo the Great, who composed them when he was the deacon of Pope Sixtus III. And later on, in his Christmas sermons, Leo never tired of reminding his hearers of the connection of the feast with the grace of baptism: "For every man who is born again, the water of baptism is the symbol of the womb of the Virgin: for it is the same Spirit that gives power to the fountain of baptism as gave power to the Virgin to conceive."[108] The power in baptism is thus foreshadowed in the power that overshadowed the Virgin: at every baptismal font the Church is there as mother, and the mother of Jesus is there. Thus in another Christmas sermon Leo says:

> The same fruitfulness which He gave to the womb of the Virgin, He has given to the fountain of baptism: He has bestowed on the water, what He bestowed on His own mother. It was the power of the Most High and the shadow of the Spirit that enabled Mary to give birth to the Redeemer: by the same power the waves of regeneration are able to give birth to the faithful.[109]

Dedit aquae quod dedit matri: in this classical statement Pope Leo has summed up the mystery connecting the Incarnation and baptism.

An unknown poet of the eighth century wrote the grand hymn which we still use for the dedication of a church, where the Church is pictured as Jerusalem, the City of Peace. But he also added a verse about the newly-baptized, which was often sung together with the hymn on Easter night in Gaul:

> *Fonte prolem salutari*
> *Chrismatis et unguine*
> *Candidatam et ornatam*
> *Virgo mater afferens,*
> *Quam superna proles Patris*
> *Christus caelo accipit.*[110]

> Children rising from the fountain,
>   Chrism-fragrant, unction-bright,
> With the Virgin, mother-caring,
>   As she brings them robed in white;
> Heaven-destined, Christ begets them,
>   Sole-begotten in the height.

And in the Middle Ages the same close connection between the Incarnation and baptism was not forgotten, as the Christmas sermon of Ivo of Chartres shows:

> This is the birth, when Christ was born into this world of time; and it is not unlike the birth, when the Christian is reborn in the spirit. For the Mother of Christ was a virgin when she conceived, a virgin when she gave birth, and remained a virgin ever after. And so it is with the Church, the bride of Christ: day by day in the water and in the word she gives birth to Christian folk, and remains a virgin ever.[111]

Let us pause here for a moment. What exactly does it mean, when the early Church speaks of the Christian's rebirth in baptism as the fulfilment of the birth of our Lord from the Virgin? In baptism we receive the supernatural gift of faith, and are disposed to charity: in a word we receive the gift of salvation, which is completed in the next life by the everlasting vision of God. "What do you ask?" is the priest's question to the candidate for baptism. And the answer is "faith." The dialogue continues: "What does faith bring thee to?" and the answer "life everlasting."

Now when with the early Christians we think of Mary present at our baptism, we are really saying no more than what Pope Leo XIII said in his Marian encyclical:

> The Fathers spoke of Mary as our Lady, our mediatrix, restorer of the whole world, bringer of divine grace; and rightly they did so, since faith is both the foundation and the crown of divine grace, through which man attains to his supernatural end in everlasting life, and rightly is a part in the attainment and development of faith in the work of salvation attributed to her who gave birth to the author of salvation; and rightly is she called blessed because of her faith.[112]

And the Pope in the same context makes his own the words of Saint Cyril of Alexandria, preached at Ephesus on the day of the solemn definition of the dogma of our Lady's divine motherhood:

> Through thee, O Mother of God, is every creature led to a knowledge of the truth; through thee are the faithful drawn to holy baptism, through thee are churches founded everywhere among the nations.[113]

Now the grace of baptism is the foundation of all subsequent graces and is the immediate and everlasting meeting-point of redeemed mankind with the redeeming God made man, who began His work of salvation with His birth from Mary. And it therefore follows in the strict symbolism of theology, that the womb of Mary is a true symbol of the baptismal font, from which Christians go forth as newborn children of God.

And thus we come to a whole world of thought, so dear to the early Church, and shared every year in the Latin liturgy of Easter night in the blessing of the font: baptism, according to the exposition given above, is thought of as a reflection of the birth of our Lord from the Virgin Mary, and similarly as a birth of our spiritual life from the Virgin that is the Church. Thus in the old Spanish liturgy of baptism on Easter night we find the text:

> The children of light go forth from baptism: tonight they are born, by the grace of the Spirit, of their mother the Church to greet a new day: without stain she conceived them, she brought them forth without pain: for she stands as a figure of the Virgin Mother of God, who without the work of man received the blessed fruit of her womb.[114]

And also on Easter night Saint Zeno of Verona cannot contain himself for joy, when he looks at his beloved children, about to be baptized, standing before him:

> Why stand you here, so various as you are by descent, in age, in sex and in calling? In a moment you will all be one. Hasten to the water, to the womb of that mother who is ever a virgin! Here is your renewal, your Resurrection, your life everlasting!

> She is the mother of all, she makes us one, she brings us together from all races and nations, and makes us henceforth into one single body![115]

And Saint Peter Chrysologus at Ravenna preaches to his catechumens about the same mystery of the motherhood of the Church. And all this becomes understandable in the light of the mystery (hardly now any more expressly so called) of the virginal motherhood of Mary. Mary and the Church are but one.

> Therefore, my brethren, when the Spirit of Heaven through His mystical light has given power to the virginal womb of this water, by this power all who are made from the dust of the earth and are born earthly, are reborn heavenly, into the likeness of their creator.[116]

Among the important evidences of this consciousness of the Marian nature of the mystery of baptism is a sermon for the baptismal feast of the Epiphany, which used to be ascribed to Augustine but is now attributed to the same Chrysologus. Here the preacher speaks in highly rhetorical terms of the comparison between the womb of Mary and the womb of the baptismal water:

> Yes, indeed we could almost say that even greater graces are given to the water of baptism than are given to Mary. For Mary merited her chastity for herself alone, while the water has brought holiness to us all. Mary merited to be without sin, while the water washes away all sin. The one was completely

free from all personal sin, while the other by God's grace forgives the sin of others. Mary gave birth to the one, and remained a virgin, while the water gives birth to many and yet remains clean. The one knew a single child in Jesus, while the other is the mother of all the nations in Christ.[117]

Of course that is rhetoric rather than theology, but it does show how vividly the early Church preached to the faithful the realization of the wonder of the grace of baptism, when it is linked with a childlike joy over the place of Mary at the font.

And so it should be with us. Our piety of today is so often dull and joyless, because we forget the origin of it all in our baptism. And at this very origin of grace stands Mary, since at baptism Christ is born in our hearts. We sing to her indeed as "our life, our sweetness and our hope," let us also sing to her as our beloved Lady of baptism.

And when we pray to her in this way, we are also greeting our beloved mother the Church, for it was from her that we were born. Yet we shall only fully understand our debt to her, how we were brought forth from the womb of the water, when all will be plain in the light of the everlasting vision of God. We were "born again of water and the Holy Spirit" (John 3:5): the power of the water derived from the Spirit, the power of which the Church sings on Easter night, the power of the Church's motherhood—and this power we can only understand if we realize that Mary is there beside the font, as symbol of the Church's motherhood:

Look down, O Lord, upon the countenance of Thy Church, and ever increase her power of rebirth.... Thou layest open to the whole world the fountain of baptism for the renewal of the nations: by Thy royal command may this fountain receive the grace of thine only-begotten Son from the Holy Spirit. May the same Spirit by the hidden presence of His own divinity give power to this water, which is destined to give new birth to mankind. And thus may a new heavenly offspring, conceived in holiness, reborn a new creature, come forth from the immaculate womb of this divine fountain... so that divine grace as a mother may bring forth all men to grow up in one spiritual childhood.[118]

Chapter Seven

Growth in Holiness

Birth is the beginning. Then comes life, and we grow up into it. And death is the end. It is the same with our rebirth: the beginning is at baptism, and we grow up in grace, and the spiritual life is an unfolding of the grace which begins at baptism, with the power of the Holy Spirit bringing us gradually more and more into the likeness of Christ: "building up the body of Christ, until we all attain to the unity of faith and of the deep knowledge of the Son of God, to perfect manhood, to the mature measure of the fullness of Christ" (Ephesians 4:12-13, Confraternity text). We are brought therefore into the life of Christ through the fullness of His manhood to His death on the cross.

And just as the new life coming from baptism comes from the womb of the Virgin, from Mary and the Church, and as earthly life derives from earthly birth, so it is with the spiritual life. There is no moment, no movement of our spiritual life that does not look back in a mystical sense to the womb whence we came. We are always experiencing the rebirth from our mother, since every turn of events in our life is in a real sense the realization, scattered through time and space, of the germ of life derived from our mother. It is in this sense that the Fathers in their theology of the spiritual life are able to say that the baptized Christian experiences day by day a new fulfilment of the birth of Christ within his heart.[119]

Asceticism and the cultivation of virtue represent the growth of Christ born of Mary, born of the Church. Preaching the Gospel and the care of souls represents that holy suffering of which Paul speaks: "My little children, of whom I am in labor again until Christ be formed in you" (Galatians 4:19).

It is of this spiritual growth of Christ in our hearts that we would now speak after having discussed our birth in baptism. What we call in general the "spiritual life" is something usually viewed as very complex, with all its questions of virtues, devotion, mortification, and so forth; but if we attempt to consider it quite simply in terms of the growth of Christ in our hearts, we shall find we are looking at one more aspect of the mystery of Mary and the Church. It will soon become both clearer and more provocative of our love, that Mary as the mother of Christ is also the mother who not only gave birth to our new life, but who protects our continued life of virtue, and who daily announces the Church's power as a mother over the growth of our spiritual lives.

The Fathers of the early Church had a special fondness for connecting this aspect of the mystery of Mary and the Church, as concerning our own growth in holiness, with a particular event in the Gospel. It is a reply of our Lord regarding His mother, which has perhaps seemed to us as strange as His reply at Cana. We all know the passage:

> And one said to Him: Behold Thy mother and Thy brethren stand without, seeking Thee. But He answering him that told Him, said: Who is My mother, and who are My brethren? And stretching forth His hand towards His disciples, He said: Behold My mother and My brethren. For whosoever shall do the will of My Father that is in heaven, he is My brother, and sister, and mother (Matthew 12:47-50).

These words, which at first sight seem to be a denial of His human and earthly relationship with His mother, are in fact the highest praise He could give His mother: for who of all mankind had so perfectly fulfilled the will of the heavenly Father as the Virgin had done, when in virtue of her *Fiat mihi* she had become the mother of the eternal Son? Furthermore, His answer implies that from now on in the Kingdom of Heaven it is His mother's *Fiat* that will find an echo in the hearts of all who do the will of the Father in following Him. And it is precisely of these His followers that Christ says that they are in a mystical sense His mother.

If therefore the Church is mystically the company of those who do the will of the Father, she is indeed Mary in the world, the mother of Christ who gives birth every day. She is indeed all that our spiritual life stands for, since this is nothing more nor less than the daily fulfilment of the will of the Father. Here is a new motherly relationship to Christ, whose desire is daily to be born in our hearts, and in us, and through us to grow to His "perfect manhood, to the mature measure of His fullness."

This in early times was the thought of the great Origen on the spiritual life: for him the Christian's life after baptism is seen as the growth of Christ Himself within the motherly hearts of the faithful: "Just as an infant is formed in the womb, so it seems to me that the Word of God is in the heart of a soul, which has received the grace of baptism and then forms within itself the word of faith ever more glorious and more plain."[120]

We spoke of this before, when considering Origen's theology of the Church as the mother of God. What was there said of the Church, is now said of the individual soul: through the life of grace which springs from baptism the soul becomes like Mary and like the

Church the "mother of the Word." In the daily birth of Christ in the Christian heart, God causes our spirit to give birth: "God opens the womb for the birth of the saints. This is to be understood in a spiritual sense: that God opens the womb of the soul, so that the Word of God should be born—and thus the soul becomes the mother of Christ."[121]

All our striving after virtue, which is what makes us Christlike, is therefore a perpetual rebirth from the womb of the virgin mother, from the Church, from Mary.

> All the baptized bear the sign, the mark, the character of Christ, the Son of man, upon them [says Methodius of Philippi] for the likeness of the Logos has been impressed upon them at their new birth. This is fulfilled in their faith and their profession, so that in each of them Christ is in a spiritual sense reborn. That is why the Church is "travailing in birth" and "in pain to be delivered" (Revelation 12:2), until Christ is formed and born within us, so that in this way each one of the saints by his sharing in Christ is once more born as Christ.[122]

There exists a sermon preached by one of the circle of the great Cappadocian Fathers who gathered round Gregory of Nazianzus: it treats of our daily struggle towards virtue, with particular reference to our Lord's words in Matthew 12:50:

> Every soul carries Christ within herself as in her womb. But if she is not transformed through a

holy life, she cannot be called Christ's mother. Yet whenever you receive Christ's word within you, and let it live in your heart, and build it up with your thoughts as in the womb, then you can be called Christ's mother.

Are you a just man? Behold, you have built up Christ within you.

Are you a generous man? Behold, you have formed within you the image of Truth itself.[123]

The interpretation of Matthew 12:50 adopted by the Fathers follows upon their consideration of the Christian's daily striving after perfection as a building up of Christ in the heart, symbolized by His birth from the Virgin Mary, and at the same time a development of the Church herself from the sacrament of baptism. Thus Gregory of Nyssa in his book of virginity:

What happened historically with the Virgin Mary, when the fullness of the Godhead in Christ Jesus shone into the world through the Virgin, is also fulfilled in every soul leading a chaste life in the manner of the Logos.[124]

And again:

This birth comes from God. And it is fulfilled every time the immortality of the spirit is conceived in the living earth of a man's heart: for then he is giving birth to wisdom, to justice, to holiness and to utter purity. Thus every Christian can become the mother of Him who is all these things essentially. For our

Lord Himself said: Whosoever shall do the will of My Father that is in heaven, he is My mother.[125]

It is from our baptism in the womb of the Church that we receive this "immortality of the spirit": henceforth it is a matter of growth in virtue, and this means that Christ must be built up and perfected within us. Gregory explains this in a profound exposition of the theology of grace in his Commentary on the Canticle:

> The child born within us is Jesus, and in each one who receives Him He grows in divers ways "in wisdom and age and grace." In divers ways in each one, according to the degree of grace in each, and according as each is ready to receive Him, He comes as a small child, as a growing boy, or as a mature man.[126]

At this point we can see how the life of Christian virtue, be it of the sinner or the saint, the newly-baptized beginner or the high mystic, has a wonderful unity in the one growing Christ. This "growth in holiness" is the growth of Christ from birth to manhood. The Christian soul has become a "Mary"—and this is a favorite thought of the great Saint Ambrose. Thus Magdalene after her conversion was addressed by our Lord simply as "Mary" (John 20:16); so it is also with the soul converted to Christ by baptism:

> When the soul then begins to turn to Christ, she is addressed as "Mary," that is, she receives the name of the woman who bore Christ in her womb: for

she has become a soul who in a spiritual sense gives
birth to Christ.[127]

Yet, even after baptism the soul is always in mortal
danger of losing this life in Christ, through sin.

Not all have brought to birth, not all are perfect,
not all are "Mary": for even though they have
conceived Christ by the Holy Spirit, they have not
all brought Him to birth. There are those who
thrust out the Word of God, as it were miscarrying.
See to it therefore that you do the will of the
Father, so that you may be the mother of Christ.[128]

When therefore we come to look upon sin after
baptism and the threat of the loss of everlasting life in
this context of the Marian mystery of the Church, we
begin to see the problem of striving after spiritual
perfection in a new light. It was above all Augustine
who pointed out this path to his hearers: he never tired
of telling them that all Christian growth in holiness,
from the merest simple possession of the faith to the
heroic heights of spiritual virginity, is in the end
nothing more than the growth of the Church in the
image of Mary.

When you look with wonder on what happened to
Mary, you must imitate her in the depths of your
own souls. Whoever believes with all his heart and
is "justified by faith" (Romans 5:1), he has conceived Christ in the womb. And whenever "with
the mouth confession is made unto salvation"

(Romans 10:10), that man has given birth to
Christ. Be you therefore overflowing with fertility
in the spirit, and at the same time unchanging in
the soul's virginity.[129]

And when addressing the consecrated virgins, who
are a living symbol of the Church's own virginity, he
says to them:

Rejoice, O virgins of Christ, for your companion is
the mother of Christ. And remember the words
which He uttered: "Whosoever shall do the will of
My Father, he is My mother." You also are therefore the mother of Christ, because you are doing
the will of the Father: you also conceive Christ
through your faith: bring Him then to birth
through your good works. And may your hearts
become filled with the law of Christ, as the womb
of Mary was filled with His body.[130]

What therefore is accomplished in individual souls,
rising through the power of baptism to the heights of
Christian virtue and perfection, is accomplished also in
and by the Church. For the Church owes her growth
to the many who become "Mary": the Church is the
one unique body of Christ, built up from birth into
manhood. So here once more, both in the growth in
holiness of individual souls and in the various developments of the life of the Church, the Church and Mary
are seen as one. There is a lovely prayer in the ancient
Spanish liturgy:

What was once bestowed upon the flesh of Mary, may this now be bestowed upon the spirit of the Church; that her unswerving faith may conceive Thee, O Christ, in the womb; that her spirit, freed from all stain of sin, may bring Thee to birth; that our own souls, overshadowed by the power of the Most High, may give Thee a mother's care. Depart not from us, but rather go forth from within us![131]

But there is yet another idea from the Fathers that fits in here, and helps to show how fundamental a notion the idea of Mary and the Church was to them. An essential feature of the Christian life, formed by the sacramental power of the grace of baptism, is that the Christian is not only striving to become Christlike himself, but to become an apostle of Christ among others, and to share with them what by Christ's gift he possesses. The Christian therefore becomes the "mother of Christ" also in the sense that he builds up Christ and brings Him to birth in the hearts of his neighbors. Saint Paul of course (Galatians 4:19) is the famous example of this. And Gregory the Great says:

He is above all the mother of Christ, who preaches the truth; for he gives birth to our Lord, who brings Him into the hearts of his hearers; and he is the mother of Christ, who through his words inspires a love of our Lord in the spirit of his neighbor.[132]

And in the Middle Ages, when men's thoughts were so constantly concerned with the apostolate, there is a word of Hrabanus Maurus in his Gloss, which was widely read and was a continuous source of encouragement: "He is My mother, says our Lord, who day by day brings Me to birth in the hearts of the faithful."[133]

And further, the Church is continually building herself up by this power to bring forth, through her word, her example and her labors; and always the Virgin Mary is there, bringing to birth the Word made flesh and giving Him a mother's care, for it was in her presence that our Lord spoke the word (Matthew 12:50): she is the symbol of the Church built up by word and work.

Indeed the Church is "Mary in the world." Wherever within the Church there is the silent growth in holiness, the striving after virtue and perfection, there our Lord is being born, there He is growing to perfect manhood, there is the "fullness of Christ," however hidden by the veils of human imperfection. Once more our Lord seems to overlook the weakness of His Church on earth, as on that other occasion with His eyes fixed on the far horizon He seemed to overlook His earthly mother as she "stood without," and waited. And what was then the most wonderful word of praise for His Mother Mary, is now a word of praise for the Church as yet unglorified on the earth: Whosoever shall do the will of My Father, he is My mother. As Haymo of Halberstadt says:

> The Church is indeed the mother of whom our Lord said: "Whosoever shall do the will of My

Father, he is My mother," for when she day by day begets new children, Christ is born within them."[134]

In this way is inspired our own love of our holy and beloved mother the Church, and we love her because she is the mother of every secret movement of the heart, every virtue, every hidden aspiration, every soaring of the spirit: in short, of every human activity that is pleasing in the sight of God, even when no man on earth knows of it. For Christ is born in her secret womb and in her travail, and in her grows to His ever-lasting glory. The mystic Richard of Saint Victor gathered these ideas together in his commentary on the woman of Revelation, and with this quotation we can end:

> The holy Church is striving with all her might to do the will of the Father, in order to become the mother of Christ. For the Church all-holy becomes Christ's mother, whenever she strives to do what is pleasing to the Father: she conceives Him in her womb through the power of grace in the faith, she gives Him birth through her holy desire, she has Him as her child through her good works.[135]

Chapter Eight

Valiant Woman

Growth in holiness is not only a continual rebirth, but it is also a toilsome journey through the years. That is life. And every step on this journey, be it upon the dusty roads of everyday tasks, be it over the hills of joy or through the nights of pain, is a step nearer the journey's end. And that is death.

And so it is with the Church's lot upon earth, and with the spiritual life of any Christian. The Church's life, and with it the life of any Christian, is a constant identification with the life of Christ. At first He walked the roads of Galilee, and then, of a sudden, without ever turning back, "He steadfastly set His face to go to Jerusalem" (Luke 9:51), there to meet His death upon the cross. And the Church follows Him upon this road, shyly, distant and unnoticed, like the woman who conceived Him in the quiet home of Nazareth, but who now follows Him along His road to the Easter festival of His death, where she came finally to be the *Mulier fortis*, the "valiant woman," standing at the foot of His cross.

In this journey through everyday life to the cross we find a new aspect of the mystery of Mary and the Church: the mystery of her inner strength amid the ordinariness of her life on earth. For only he who can prove his unswerving faithfulness to Christ by his powerful patience in everyday life, is able to go with Christ to Calvary and to share His joy in the Resurrection. The test comes between Nazareth and Golgotha: it was the test for Mary, it is the test for the Church and for each one of us.

The classical passage in praise of this strength in Mary and in the Church, cited by the Fathers and mystics, is the poem of the valiant woman at the end of the Book of Proverbs (Proverbs 31:10-31):

> Who shall find a valiant woman? Far and from the uttermost coasts is the price of her. The heart of her husband trusteth in her.... She hath sought wool and flax, and hath wrought by the counsel of her hands. She is like the merchant's ship: she bringeth her bread from afar.... Her lamp shall not be put out in the night. She hath put out her hand to strong things: and her fingers have taken hold of

the spindle. She hath opened her hand to the needy, and stretched out her hands to the poor....

The history of the interpretation of the valiant woman by the Fathers of the early Church and the mystics of the early Middle Ages is one of the special treasures of the theology of Mary and the Church.[136] The Fathers saw in the song of the valiant woman above all an application to the Church, our mother; so much so, in fact, that their interpretation gave rise in medieval times to the tenderest expressions of love of our Lady, the woman who in herself includes all the mysteries of the Church. And at the same time they saw the symbolism of our own sanctification: for the figure of the valiant woman is fulfilled not only in our Lady and in the Church, but also in ourselves, since (to use the phrase of Ambrose) by our baptism we become not only "Mary," but are identified with the Church. Thus a mystic of the school of Bernard of Clairvaux sees Mary, the Church, and the soul all in one:

> Under the figure of the valiant woman we can see Mary, the mother of divine wisdom, or the Church, the mother of the wise, or the soul, which is where wisdom resides.[137]

Let us look now more closely at the valiant woman as symbolizing both Mary and the Church on the road from Nazareth to Golgotha. The beginning is at the moment of the Incarnation in the heart of Mary, at the supreme instant of her acceptance of the task, when she became the mother of the Word. The precious blood that was to redeem the world was her blood, and in this way her road was already marked out, the road through those everyday years, leading direct to Golgotha.

It is to this mystery of her life, and her life already at Nazareth, where "love is strong as death" (Canticles 8:6), that the Cistercian mystic refers, when he sees in the moment of the Incarnation the fulfilment of the valiant woman:

> A Lady full of bravery: she traveled through her mortal life upon this evil world, yet through the majesty of her spirit she surpassed all creation. For it was to her, the valiant woman, that Gabriel was sent—his very name means "God's valiant man." Was she not indeed valiant, this woman, Mary, whose love was stronger than death?

For her acceptance of the Incarnation was the acceptance of death. Her blood she gave Him, only for Him to shed it. And this also is fulfilled in the Church: the Church, like Mary, is the woman who brings Christ into the world, only to be sacrificed upon the altar. Incarnation and death are made one in the Church's sacraments, for in the sacrificial death, Christ's Body is every day reborn. Thus the symbol of the valiant woman is fulfilled also in the Church and her vocation on earth: valiant indeed is this great woman of the world, since as the mystical mother of

Christ crucified, daily she meets death again. This acceptance of death, in which she follows Mary, is verified in her day-to-day history, her persecutions, and her daily cares. In this she is truly valiant. This is what Epiphanius of Salamis once told his people:

> You are the children of that wise and valiant woman, of whom Solomon said: "Who shall find a valiant woman?" This valiant woman, is she not the Church, your mother? For none is braver than she, who every time a persecution is raised against her is ready to go to death for the name of her beloved.[138]

Another verse of the poem of the valiant woman brings us still deeper into the mystery of Mary and the Church: "She is like the merchant's ship: she bringeth her bread from afar." Mary has indeed brought our Lord to the world "from afar," from the height of His eternity. And it was at Bethlehem, that is, in "the house of bread," that she gave birth to Him who said of Himself: "I am the living bread, which came down from heaven ... I am the bread of life" (John 6:51,48). Christ is the bread of Bethlehem, that changes the famine of sin into a feast of joy, the treasure from the Father's heavenly storehouse, which enriches all mankind.

The Fathers liked to think of the valiant woman as a richly-laden ship, sailing from afar and bringing victuals and great treasure. Mary is this ship, they said, and the babe of Bethlehem is the bread and the treasure. Ephrem the Syrian in one of his lovely songs to our Lady says:

> She is a ship, laden with priceless treasures, which has brought heavenly riches to the poor. The dead have received gifts from her, who had carried life itself within her.[139]

The ship of blessing comes indeed from afar: from the Father's House Mary, the valiant woman, has brought her treasure. There is still in the Maronite liturgy of today a beautiful passage, written in the fifth century by Jacob of Batnae: "Mary is the ship bringing good treasure from the House of the Father, to scatter His riches in our desolate land."[140]

And there are echoes through the ages of that tender Syriac devotion to our Lady, based on this verse of the poem of the valiant woman; in particular there is the lovely carol so well known in German speaking lands, *Es kommt ein Schiff geladen* by Tauler, the mystic, where Tauler writes of our Lady as the valiant woman, under the figure of the ship.

Auf einem stillen Wege	A little ship is sailing
kommt uns das Schiffelin,	The silent waves between,
es bringt uns reiche Gabe	The richest gift she brings us,
die Herren-Konigin.	Of all the world the Queen.
Das Schifflein das geht stille	The sweetest gift she brings us
und bringt uns reiche Last,	In silence sailing past,
das Segel ist die Minne,	Her mainsail is a love-song,
der Heilig Geist der Mast.[141]	The Holy Ghost her mast.

That is a genuine echo of the ancient theology of
the Fathers about the Church. She, together with Mary,
is the valiant woman, who, like a ship coming from
afar and laden with gifts, brings heavenly riches to im-
poverished mankind. Already in the fourth century the
ship in our poem was taken to represent the Church:

> There is no doubt that this ship is a symbol of the
> Church, as the Holy Spirit has said through
> Solomon: "She is like a merchant's ship, coming
> from afar." That is the Church, which impelled by
> the breath of the Holy Spirit sails upon every sea,
> laden with treasure ineffably precious, the blood of
> Christ, by which all mankind and even the whole
> cosmos itself is redeemed.[142]

In Mary and in the Church the destitute world
becomes rich, and starving mankind is fed lavishly.

It is in the mystery of the blood of Christ, prepared
by Mary in the flesh, and scattered sacramentally by
the Church, that the day-to-day perseverance of the
valiant woman is recognized. When Mary accepted the
motherhood of the Redeemer, she not only accepted
His death, but also the daily trials throughout life, in
particular the more and more frequent and more and
more painful loss of her child and parting from Him
during His life on earth, a kind of daily death during
those last years, and her enforced solitude and hidden
life, her complete loss of Him in the fullness of His
manhood, her retirement into obscurity—and all the

time a truly motherly readiness to be at hand when the terrible trial of the death of her son began.

And the same pattern is seen in the Church: her whole history is a meeting with death, she is forced into retirement, despised and forgotten, and yet has an ever-present anxiety about her heart's beloved child: in a word, she is a true mother.

Augustine once preached a wonderful sermon to his people, and he went straight to their hearts when he interpreted the valiant woman of the Church: "Whenever you hear this text, I know you at once think this must be the Church," he begins, and he then goes on to develop the idea: "the valiant woman is indeed the Church, the mother of the martyrs, who rises in the dark night of history to provide victuals, who weaves wool and flax, whose lamp is never put out." And then he depicts her on earth in terms of the text: "Here below she is always at work, alert, anxious, careful about the state of her house; at night she is up and about, seeing that the lamp is still burning; when trouble comes she is ready to face it, she is ever careful to provide for the future; and all the time she is busy, her spindle is never still, not even at her mealtimes is she idle."[143]

There indeed is Mary in the world. And whenever, in the history of her trials, the Church does not fulfill this ideal image of the valiant woman, she is no longer the mother of Christ, for her whole work is the pilgrimage from Nazareth to Golgotha. Thus Adam of

Perseigne, in his great sermon on the Assumption, based upon the text of the valiant woman, describes the Church as the fulfilment of Mary:

> Her toil is in her manifold birthgiving and in her distress of sighing. Hers are the "pains as of a woman in labor" (Psalm 47:7). Her loving care is for the holy children, whom she conceived by the Holy Spirit, for them the warmth of her love, for them her motherly concern and untold sorrow over the dangers and temptations which assail them.[144]

Here we touch upon a new Marian mystery in the Church: the mystery of her daily life and her history of pain.

> The valiant woman is the holy Catholic Church. Woman she is called, because she has brought forth spiritual children to God by water and the Holy Spirit. Valiant she is called, because she disdains and despises all pains and yearnings of this world, for the sake of her true love for her creator and redeemer.[145]

Thus it is—or at least, thus it should be—with our mother the Church. And it rests with us, her children, her members, who are she herself, whether this Marian mystery of the valiant woman is verified in the world or not. All our meditation so far has been on Mary and the Church in the ideal order, and similarly our thoughts of the woman who represents our own spiritual lives. It rests with us, through our own training of ourselves and our own effort, to make our lives every day a pilgrimage, from the Nazareth of our baptism to the Golgotha of our union with the suffering Christ. The strong faith deep in our own hearts, our daily struggle towards perfection, our earnest wait for the glorious coming of the Lord: this is our pilgrimage. As Ambrose says, we must become an *anima ecclesiastica*, a soul identified with the Church. The holy doctor uses this phrase again, when he applies the text of the valiant woman to the Christian soul. And may these words from the early centuries be a reminder to us struggling Christians of today:

> And thou, O soul who believest in God, shouldst be a valiant woman! For Solomon is speaking of the soul that is one with the Church, or of the Church herself, when he says: "Who shall find a valiant woman?" More than of most precious jewels is the price of her. "The heart of her husband trusteth in her." She lifts up her hands in the night-time, she weighs in the balance her goods justly gained. Moderation and measure are hers in all things. Ever anxious she waits for her husband, longing and yearning for his return and to be with him, saying in her heart: "My lord is long a-coming" (Matthew 24:48), but I will up and go to meet him and greet him face to face, when he begins to come in his majesty. "Come, Lord Jesus" (Revelation 22:20), Thou shall never find Thy bride disfigured or defiled, never has she dishonored Thy house or

forgotten Thy commands, but with joy she comes to meet Thee: "I found Him whom my soul loveth" (Canticles 3:4).[146]

It is this true love that is the proof. It is at the spindle of our everyday tasks that we learn to meet Christ crucified, and on the cross we find the measure of our love for Christ victorious. It is in the pattern of our daily life that we can discern the shape of our eternity. But it is on the road to Jerusalem that Mary meets her child once more, now risen from the dead, and henceforth it is joy without end. And therefore the poem of the valiant woman ends [in the Septuagint text] with the significant verse: "And in the city-gates her husband shall be praised." Augustine has a famous passage on this text, applying both to the Church and to our own lives, when eventually the everyday turns into the eternal:

> Where is this city-gate? It is where our earthly toils have their end, and everlasting vision and praise of God begin. No more shall it be said to the valiant woman: Up and to work! Lay out the wool and tend the lamp; quick, arise in the night, look after the poor, busy thy spindle and distaff! No more of that labor for thee, yet never shalt thou be idle: for now everlasting thy vision shall be, fulfilling thy heart's long desire, praising Him without end. For here, at the gates of eternity, thy spouse shall be praised forever.[147]

Chapter Nine

The Pledge of the
Spirit in Our Hearts

We have been on the road with the mother of Jesus, from Nazareth to Golgotha. Her life is a symbol of the Church's mystery, for all through the ages this "valiant woman" has been journeying, from the mystical birth of Christ to His mystical death: from the water of baptism to the altar of sacrifice.

But birth and death, in both Mary and the Church, have their supreme fulfilment: everything is hastening towards the day when the Holy Spirit comes, bringing life and light and fire from heaven: Pentecost. For this is the day when the Mystical Body of Christ, the Church, was conceived; the anticipation of what is to come at the end of days upon all the redeemed, within the womb of their mother the Church: "And it shall come to pass in the last days (saith the Lord), I will pour out of My Spirit upon all flesh" (Acts 2:17). Only then will it be revealed what was the ultimate end of God becoming man and dying on the cross: the rebirth in Christ of mankind now glorious forever. And behold, at this hour too, "the mother of Jesus was there" (John 2:1). Mary is there at the Church's beginning.

Mary's presence at Pentecost is the last view we have of her in the writings of revelation: henceforth she disappears into the twilight that followed the glory of her son's Ascension. But her gentle, humble and motherlike retirement is once more full of significance, for they were all "persevering with one mind in prayer with the women, and Mary, the mother of Jesus, and with His brethren" (Acts 1:14).

During those days after our Lord's Ascension, days of anxious waiting for the Spirit which He had promised them at His departure, the mother of Jesus is the center of the little company which was the beginning of the Church. "She who had given life to God made man, has a special part to play at the birth of His Mystical Body."[148] Beloved of the early Middle Ages was the lovely comment of the Gloss: "Behold, this is the beginning of the Church, now about to be born, and she is adorned with the flower of virginity!"[149]

And Arator, a poet of the sixth century, when he told the story of the Acts of the Apostles in verse, has a

delicate description of the Apostles returning to the
gates of the Holy City after the Ascension: to the gates
of the city where the Spirit was so soon to come upon
them, but in a mystical sense to the gate, whence Christ
who is sending the Spirit comes forth to meet them,
that is, to Mary the mother of the Church. The holy
Virgin, he says, is the gate, and now all the Apostles and
their friends are gathered round her: this is the Church's
beginning, containing the beginning and the end in one,
conception and Pentecost and the birth of mankind's
new life of the spirit: "Mary is God's gateway, the
spotless mother of her creator, created by her own son.
The second virgin canceled the sin of Eve, and through
her came the Mediator into the world, and took our
flesh to the height of heaven."[150]

Let us now look more carefully into the mystery of
the descent of the Holy Spirit, and see its connection
with that of Mary and the Church. We have called this
chapter "The Pledge of the Spirit in our Hearts" quoting
from 2 Corinthians 1.22, since Pentecost was the
beginning of what will be fulfilled at the end of days,
"because the charity of God is poured forth in our
hearts, by the Holy Spirit who is given to us" (Romans
5:5), and we have "received the spirit of adoption of
sons, whereby we cry: Abba (Father)" (Romans 8:15).

Here indeed is fulfilled in all mankind what was
begun in the heart of the Virgin at the instant of the
Incarnation: in the sanctuary of her immaculate heart,

in her innermost being, in her trusting and obedient spirit, in her spotless womb, when the overshadowing grace of the Holy Spirit came in. The heart of Mary is the beginning of the story: in her heart was performed in secret, what now at Pentecost is open to the gaze of all mankind. The heart of Mary is the original upper room, where redeemed mankind is gathered.

Saint Augustine never tired of emphasizing this mystery: "Mary's loving motherhood would indeed have profited little, had she not first conceived Christ in her heart, and only then in her womb."[151] Pentecost has its origin in the innermost heart of Mary: it was there the Church was born. Her assent at the Annunciation is the foundation of all that was to come. "We can imagine her as saying: now there will be born of an immaculate virgin, by the power of the Holy Spirit, the one from whom will then be born, by the same Holy Spirit, the immaculate Church."[152]

We shall penetrate more intimately the mystery of the Church, if we consider the mystery of the heart of Mary. Twice Saint Luke speaks of her heart, as it were indicating his source: "Mary kept these words, pondering them in her heart," and "His mother kept all these words in her heart" (Luke 2:19, 51). For it was above all from her that the Church learned of the mysteries of the childhood of Jesus:

> O thou truly wise mother, alone worthy of such a
> son! All these words she pondered in her heart,

keeping them for us, so that later they might be spoken and preached throughout the world. For the Apostles learned all these things from her."[153]

But there is a still deeper meaning: Mary "pondered" these things in her heart. Gradually Mary grew to an even fuller understanding of God's word, and of how all that had been foretold by the prophets was now being fulfilled in her own heart, thence to be reflected into the future. The great Origen was already preaching about this: "Mary kept the words of Christ in her heart, kept them as a treasure, knowing that the time would come, when all that was hidden within her would be revealed."[154]

Mary became a prophet in her heart, simply because "in her spirit she held the divine, and in her heart she was united to God."[155] Augustine calls her the fulfilment of all the prophets.[156] A mystic of the Middle Ages sees in his own way how the chaste sanctuary of Mary's heart is the fulfilment of all prophecies, and the center where all the words of God, like so many different rays, converge.[157] And an ancient fragment of the literature of the Greek Church explains the words of Saint Luke in the same way: "Everything that our Lord said was treasured by Mary as the most sacred possession and hidden in the depths of her heart, for she realized that His words were as it were the seeds, the audible signs of things to come, utterly divine and ineffable."[158]

Amid these thoughts we recognize what we rightly

call the "devotion to the sacred heart of Mary," already with the Fathers and the writers of the Middle Ages. An early Greek theologian speaks of the heart of Mary as "the sacred vessel of all mysteries."[159] For into her heart came the Spirit with a fullness that filled it to human capacity. Her heart is the *vas spirituale*, the vessel filled by the Spirit. Therefore we find her again at the foot of the cross, when the blood of Christ was shed, the blood of her heart, when He "through the Holy Spirit offered Himself" (Hebrews 9:14).

An important manifestation of this "theology of the heart" is noticeable in the ivories of the Carolingian age: next to the cross we see represented the majestic figure of the *Ecclesia*, receiving in a golden chalice the blood from our Lord's heart, but behind her, as a twin figure with the Church, stands Mary with hands outstretched in a motherly gesture, as if to say: This is the blood, now giving the Spirit to the Church, which is the blood formed in my heart, and in virtue of which I am the mother of the Mystical Christ.[160] In the same way there stands therefore on the other side of the cross the figure of the Synagogue, symbol of the people of God, unfaithful to the old promise. She is represented as about to flee from the sight of the cross, for now in virtue of the precious blood, a new testament in the Holy Spirit has been entrusted to the Church that is Mary. Sedulius, poet of Christian antiquity, has described in graceful hexameters this division of Synagogue and Church before the cross and the Resurrection:

Discedat synagoga suo fuscata colore
Ecclesiam Christus pulchro sibi junxit amore,
Haec est conspicuo radians in honore Mariae:
Quae cum clarifico semper sit nomine mater,
Semper virgo manet.[161]

Get thee gone, Synagogue, with thy shamed face blushing
    so darkly,
Christ and the Church are now in love everlasting united,
And she shines with a light that is radiant with honor to
    Mary:
Graced she too evermore with the privileged name of a
    mother
Always virgin remains.

And when the art of the early Church or of the Middle Ages comes to represent the Ascension and places Mary as a praying *Orante* among the Apostles, or places her among those who received the Holy Spirit in the upper room at Pentecost, one main idea is expressed: she is the woman with her heart filled by the Spirit, the mother who is the Church, and is like to Mary.[162] In her are all prophecies fulfilled, in her begins the life of heavenly glory, in her the Spirit already breathes, which shall change the world in the last days. Everything has its beginning in the heart of Mary, and in her womb. This was the meaning of the medieval mystic who saw the heart of Mary as the symbol at once of the "Church of the past," that is, of the Synagogue with the promises she received from God, and at the same

time of the "Church of the future," which from Pentecost
to the end of the world remains the bearer of the word
of God:

> Thus the Virgin Mary represents all that is noblest
> in the "Church of the past," and thereby became
> the symbol of the "Church of the future" since it
> was by the power of the Holy Spirit that God's
> only son became man in her womb, and by the
> power of the same Holy Spirit many sons were to
> be born to God from the womb of the Church,
> through the lifegiving waters of His grace.[163]

And the same mystic can show us more of the
mystery of the heart of Mary, full of the Spirit, showing us at the same time more of the mystery of the
heart of the Church, our mother. Mary is indeed the
"valiant woman," journeying from Nazareth to Golgotha and thence to the upper room at Pentecost,
reaching there the very heart of her share in the work
of Redemption. Thus she became the symbol of the
Mater Ecclesia. "But who is the valiant woman?" asks
the mystic. "We know she is the Church," he answers,
and then continues:

> Let us, however, ask a further question. How can
> we speak of so many races, in so many centuries,
> such a crowd of souls of men, as one "woman," one
> single *Ecclesia* made up of so many, one woman of
> whom it is said that "the heart of her husband
> trusteth in her"? There is but one answer, it seems
> to me: the unity of the faith.

That is, then, the heart of the mystery of the Virgin Mary and the virgin Church: her faith. Her humble obedience of the heart, the opening of her heart in love, her complete trust in the Spirit that overshadowed her. And the same mystic explains this great truth in the light of the phrase from the poem of the valiant woman: "The heart of her husband trusteth in her" (Proverbs 31:11).

> Let us search the text more closely [he says], for it does not say merely "her husband trusteth in her," but "the heart of her husband trusteth in her." There is a place and time when this can in all truth be said: it is a searching word of love, a word that searches our inmost Spirit: "The heart of her husband trusteth in her." And when was this? Truly in the inmost soul of the Virgin Mary. It was here that her spouse trusted her and opened His heart to her.
>
> And how did He open His heart? A great and ineffable mystery: for here in her inmost soul He fulfilled the words of David: *Eructavit cor meum verbum bonum*—"My heart hath uttered a good word" (Psalm 44:2).
>
> He opened His heart to her, so that the very being of His own Word, springing from His heart, His own Word, conceived in His heart before all eternity, should come into the Spirit and into the womb of a trusting virgin: a virgin who through her faith in this mystery at the instant of the angel's word conceived in her womb.[164]

This is the power that formed the Church, at work since Pentecost, but beginning its work in the inmost heart of Mary: the faith that builds up the body of Christ. In the hidden mystery of her faith the heart of God meets the heart of man in an ineffable meeting. In the midst of her heart, eternity entered time.

Here a vital question for our own spiritual life arises: is my own heart open to receive the Spirit? Is my heart a trusting heart? Is my heart a vessel ready to receive the Spirit poured out by the risen Christ? In other words, do I fully realize in my heart the meaning of the Incarnation and the gift of Pentecost? And this again can be resolved by the simple question: Is the mother of Jesus there? My understanding of the trusting heart of Mary is the measure of my love for the Church.

Saint Ambrose makes very plain this relationship between love of our Lady and love of the Church, when he is speaking of the heart of Mary, who "kept all these words" spoken by the shepherds on Christmas night "in her heart" (Luke 2:19):

> If Mary kept all these words she had learnt from the shepherds, and pondered them in her heart, why are you unwilling to learn from the priests? And if Mary kept silence until the Apostles had spoken, why do you always wish, after the Apostles have spoken, rather to teach than to learn?[165]

Here we have devotion to the heart of Mary spoken of quite simply, and even sternly, in terms of a plain, loving obedience to the Church; for after all; such an obedience is the ultimate test of love of the Church. It is only the obedient heart that is open to the grace of the Spirit. And only in the teaching voice of the Church will the eternal word of God come to us. But it is precisely by this loving and ready trust that Christ is built up: in the womb of the Virgin Mary, in the womb of the Church, and in the womb of my own heart.

"Blessed art thou that hast believed" (Luke 1:45). These words were addressed first to Mary, but they apply equally to the Church and to my own heart. And Saint Ambrose explains them in this way:

> Blessed are you also, because you have believed and have listened. For every believing soul conceives and gives birth to the Word of God. Would therefore that the soul of Mary could dwell in your hearts, to praise God! Yet, although according to the flesh one alone is the mother of Christ, according to faith all of us can give Him birth, since every soul conceives the Word of God, when stainless and free from sin. Every soul therefore thus engaged praises God as did the heart of Mary, when she said "my soul doth magnify the Lord, and my spirit hath rejoiced in God my Savior" (Luke 1:46-47).[166]

"The pledge of the Spirit in our hearts" (2 Corinthians 1:22), and loving trust: here are the foundations of the revelation, realized first in Mary and then in the Church. The same Holy Spirit which filled the heart of

Mary since Pentecost has been poured forth into the hearts of the faithful, even though perhaps in a hidden and silent way, yet mysteriously transforming. Once more Mary and the Church are one.

And this is the deep significance of the present fact, that in our own days when the love of the Church is so freshly flourishing, the devotion to the immaculate heart of Mary, filled by the Spirit, should be so specially recommended by the Holy Father Pope Pius XII, a true follower of Peter, who had preached on that first Pentecost day, saying: "This Jesus... exalted by the right hand of God, and receiving from the Father the promise of the Holy Spirit... has poured forth this Spirit which you see and hear" (Acts 2:33, Confraternity text). Indeed, the ideas we have been trying to find among the treasures of the early Church about the Spirit in the heart of Mary, Pope Pius XII has summarized at the end of his encyclical on the Mystical Body:

> We have without hesitation consecrated all mankind to the immaculate heart of Mary. May she, the most holy Mother of all members of Christ, radiant now, body and soul in heaven, and gloriously reigning with her Son, earnestly implore of Him, that mighty streams of grace may ceaselessly flow from the majestic head upon all members of the Mystical Body.[167]

Chapter Ten

The Woman of Revelation

Now we reach the last stage on earth—and indeed the first stage in heaven—of our study of our Lady as essential symbol of the Church. Even the quiet retirement of the Mother of God from the biblical scene after Pentecost, the fact that no more words of hers are recorded, the historical obscurities that involve her death and final homecoming, all these things are full of significance for the Church, and for the hidden spiritual life of each of us. But this moment is far from being the end of Mary's life: it is rather the beginning, the start of a new life, or more exactly, the true and proper existence in heaven of the Mother of God made man. Now in her new life above she has a powerful influence on earthly affairs, and is at last revealed as what she truly is. Mary, in a way corresponding to the glorious risen life of our Lord, has been transformed into a being that is of both heaven and earth; no longer now the "handmaid," for "behold from henceforth all generations shall call me blessed." And it is the same with the Church. The Church's history on earth is already a heavenly mystery: for she is always on the point of extinction, frequently persecuted, ever having to pay the toll of human weakness and death during her earthly wandering: she is truly the "handmaid" in human history. But it is precisely in this that her glory is revealed, for she also from henceforth is called blessed by all generations who spring from her fruitful womb. It is in her daily death on earth, that she shows her immortality.

The theology of the early Church regards the Virgin Mary and the Church as one, and it is when the earthly level is abandoned for the heavenly that the sublimest passages are written, based upon the great woman of Revelation:

> And a great sign appeared in heaven: a woman clothed with the sun, and the moon under her feet, and on her head a crown of twelve stars. And being with child, she cried travailing in birth, and was in pain to be delivered.... And she brought forth a man-child, who was to rule all nations with an iron rod: and her son was taken up to God, and to His throne (Revelation 12:1, 2, 5).

This vision represented Mary, Christ's Mother, who at the foot of the cross had been entrusted to the Seer of Patmos, but only insofar as she is at the same time a symbol of the Church and the Church's fate that is both earthly and heavenly. It is only in this way that we can resolve the occasional apparent contradictions in the vision: she is clothed with the sun in her heavenly glory and yet is in the pains of childbirth: she has already entered heaven and yet is still on the painful journey here below: she is at once the gracious queen and the sorrowful mother. Herein also lies the symbol of the deepest meaning of our own spiritual lives, which are always at the same time journeying and at journey's end, effort and achievement, sorrow and joy: "we are now the sons of God, and it hath not yet appeared what we shall be" (1 John 3:2).

Let us now consider the picture of the woman of Revelation, this Marian mystery of the Church, in the light of the theology of the early Church, and apply it also to our own spiritual lives.

The woman of Revelation was from the beginning a much loved picture of the Church, without emphasis on the particular application to our Lady. Hippolytus, the earliest exegetical writer of the Church of Rome, already at the end of the second century writes: "There is no doubt that the woman clothed with the sun, for Saint John means the Church. For she is clothed with the Logos, begotten of the Father, who therefore shines more brightly than the sun."[168] The Church, appearing under the figure of the woman in heaven, is for him also the "company of the saints,"[169] whose most precious possession is the garment that is the sun, the garment of the New Testament, the revelation of the eternal Word, or that is even Christ Himself, the "sun of justice" (Malachi 4:2). The power derived from being clothed with the sun of eternity makes the Church the mother of all nations, brought together into the Mystical Body of Christ. Already on this earth that is a heavenly power, it is the entrance of eternity into this world, it is the pledge of life-after-death, a pledge that is redeemed through the Church.

At this point Hippolytus continues with the thought that we quoted before, when we were considering the Church as mystically the "mother of Christ." "The Church never ceases to bring forth the Logos... the man-child who was to rule all nations... the perfect man that is Christ, the child of God."[170] This heavenly birth, brought in amidst the daily dying on earth, occurs in the mystery of baptism, when man is bathed in the sunshine of Christ, when the Church casts over the nations her mantle that is the sun. "The woman stands for the Church, and the sun stands for Christ. And the Church is clothed with the sun, because the faithful, who are the Church, have 'put on Christ' in baptism, as the Apostle says (Galatians 3:27)."[171]

Every sacrament is a mysterious borderline between heaven and earth. Now already the Church is the woman in heaven: "And a great sign appeared in heaven." The great theologian Methodius writes of this already at the end of the age of persecution, early in the fourth century, when he has an almost platonic view of the Church as a kind of heavenly archetype of our own life of grace:

> Indeed this is she, our Mother, the great woman in heaven. This is the powerful heavenly archetype, greater than all her children. This is the Church; and her children, born through baptism in all parts of the world, die on the earth but rise again and hasten to join their mother. Mark now her progress majestic, the Lady exalted in wonderful splendor, spotless and pure, and bright as the stars of the sky. For she has been clothed by Him, whose essence is light everlasting.[172]

It is interesting to notice that Methodius takes special care to reject the interpretation of this chapter with reference to Mary, the Mother of God[173]—which at any rate is evidence that the double significance of the vision was already current in his time. Indeed, since the fourth century this Marian ecclesiology is always traceable among the Greeks.[174] And in the Latin West we find a disciple of Saint Augustine addressing his newly-baptized as follows: "The woman of Revelation represents the Virgin Mary, who chastely gave birth to our chaste head, and is therefore a symbol of the Church. And as Mary, after giving birth to a son, remained a virgin, so also the Church has in every age given birth to the members of Christ, without ever losing her virginity."[175] Henceforth the Western Church of the early Middle Ages has never failed to see the Church in Mary, and Mary in the Church. And here indeed is the beginning of that tender love of our Lady, which, unlike a later age, never forgot the truly theological mystery of Mary. Alcuin, the brilliant theologian of Charlemagne's court, wrote in his commentary on Revelation:

> The Woman clothed with the sun is the Blessed Virgin Mary, who was overshadowed by the power of the Most High. But in her we can also understand the race of men that is the Church, who is not called "woman" to suggest weakness, but on the contrary because of her strength in daily bringing to birth new peoples to build up the Body of Christ. The Church, then, is "clothed with the sun," according to the word of Scripture: "As many of you as have been baptized in Christ have put on Christ" (Galatians 3:27), for Christ is "the sun of justice" (Malachi 4:2) and "the brightness of eternal light" (Wisdom 7:26).[176]

All that was foretold by the prophets of Mary and fulfilled in her life on earth, is yet more deeply realized within the Church, the company of those gathered together in Christ. Thus Haymo of Halberstadt indicates this in the ninth century:

> The great "sign" of Revelation is at the same time the "sign" that was given to Ahaz (Isaiah 7:14), a great sign indeed: "a virgin shall conceive and bear

a son" and yet remain a virgin. And moreover, the sign "appeared in heaven," that is, in the Church, of which the Mother of the Lord is also a member. For the Blessed Mother of God is here a symbol of the Church, and day by day this sign is verified in the Church, since day by day within her Christ is conceived and brought to birth.[177]

But at the beginning of the early Middle Ages the ideas of Mary and of the Church began to be separated, and a tender human cult of our Lady sprang up quite distinct from a merely legal view of the Church; yet at the same time the holy monk Rupert of Deutz could still write:

The woman clothed with the sun is the symbol of the Church, of which the most important and the best element is the Blessed Virgin Mary, because of the blessed fruit of her womb.[178]

Thus in the picture of the woman of Revelation we find gathered together all the mysteries which we have been studying one by one. With the birth of God from a woman, the womb of eternity was opened; and all the history of the Church through the centuries is but the gradual reinstatement through humility of the race of Adam, the birth of the mystical Christ, the silent yet ever-present dawning of the glory of heaven.

But this is only one aspect of the apocalyptic scene. We must look for Mary and the Church not only in the woman clothed with the sun, for there are other elements in the vision: "The moon under her feet," and "she cried, travailing in birth."

At this point the early interpreters, both Greek and Latin, came up against a difficulty in explaining the text of our Lady. "For not everything in the vision can be literally applied to the Blessed Virgin alone—much of it applies rather to the elect within the Church," says Haymo of Halberstadt.[179]

Now the woman is not only heavenly, but always belongs also to this earth: she is in labor at childbirth, she cries out in pain, she is pursued by the dragon, she takes refuge in the desert, where she looks up helplessly to her child who has been taken away to the throne of God. All this, of course, applies most obviously to the lot of the Church suffering on earth, but it was already symbolized in Mary's sufferings on earth, and is further verified in our personal trials and pains, and in the secret struggle heavenwards of our own spiritual lives in this world.

The theology of the Fathers saw this part of the symbolism especially in "the moon under her feet."[180] Just as the moon, the luminary of the night, shines only with the light of the sun, is always waxing and waning, and is darkest when nearest the sun, so is it with the Church upon earth. It is in the pain of her waning, in the darkness of her new moon, that she is nearest to Christ, and then waxes with His light to the full moon of her Eastertide and Resurrection. For this is a law of her life upon earth: she must die in order to live, she must labor in order to give birth, she must pass through the darkness in order to shine with everlasting light. Thus Saint Cyril of Alexandria, explaining the symbolism of the moon: "Sing we then a song of praise at the death of the Church, for this is a death that leads to the springs of life, the life that is holy and in Christ."[181] And he continues:

> Whenever you hear the word "Church," you know that one is speaking of the holy company of the faithful. And the death of her is the entrance to life, where we shall find citizenship with Christ; the death of her is the turning-point of transformation into a better life, far better than anything created.[182]

This therefore means that the noble Lady who is the Church has truly got the moon at her feet, for gradually and painfully she rises above everything that is of this earth; she must decrease, so that Christ, the sun, may increase; she must journey towards the everlasting light, which is only found through darkness over the earth and the sufferings of this life. The Anglo-Saxon Bede interprets the woman standing on the moon in this way:

> "A woman clothed with the sun, and the moon under her feet": this is the Church. Girded as she is with the sunshine of Christ, all earthly light she treads underfoot. The words of the Psalm are hers: "In his days shall justice spring up, and

abundance of peace, till the moon be taken away" (Psalm 71:7). This means that abundance of peace will grow, until this changeable mortality is removed, "and the enemy, death, shall be destroyed last" (1 Corinthians 15:26).[183]

This is why the Church is ever in travail, and "in pain to be delivered," and then in anxiety for her children; and why she is pursued by the dragon to the end of time. And it is the same with the struggles of our spiritual lives: the Christian is also in travail, the forming of the image of Christ in his heart is a process involving much pain, since only by dying every day can we receive God's life within us. "The pains refer also to the Holy Spirit, for in Him the saints become one sacred body and suffer pains thereby," says Hippolytus of Rome.[184] And Methodius: "Therefore the Church lies in travail, until Christ is formed within us and born of us, since each of us, by sharing in Christ, is born again as Christ, and each one is baptized in Christ into fellowship with the Spirit."[185] Throughout the Middle Ages a phrase was remembered, that was ascribed to Augustine but belongs to Gennadius of Marseilles: "The Church in painful childbirth is ever giving birth to us her members."[186]

Now if these things apply principally to the Church, they must somehow also apply to our Lady. She has indeed given birth to the Mystical Body of Christ, and this was not without pain. Indeed on our account she suffered as no mother on earth has suffered. "She cried": this also was applied in the Middle Ages by the devout Hugh of Saint Cher to Mary: "And she cried out in the pain of her innermost heart, when she came to her martyrdom at the Passion of her son."[187] And this continual birth of her mystical child continues into her life in heaven, as it were, in her painless pains of motherly anxiety about her child that is the Church. "Mary is the best, the chosen member of all the Church, her noblest daughter. Therefore she is ever anxious to bring Christ her child to birth in the souls of all the faithful, and this anxiety of hers increases to the end of time": this is the interpretation of Cornelius a Lapide, of the Marian mystery of the woman of Revelation, pursued by the dragon and crying out in travail.[188]

With the mention of "the end of time" we touch upon the fact, at once so difficult to understand but yet so evident in history, that the cult of our Lady and the tender devotion to her, which has grown throughout the ages of the Church, is closely connected with the end of the world. It is then indeed, in the grim last days, when all disasters are at hand and the dragon fights his last war against God, that the role of the victorious woman, the sign in heaven, will be fully revealed. Then will the story, begun at the gates of paradise lost, be concluded within the Church at the gates of paradise regained. Then the woman will crush the head of the serpent forever. "And that great dragon was cast out, that old serpent who is called the devil and Satan, who seduceth the whole world.... And I heard a loud voice in heaven, saying: Now is come salvation, and strength, and the kingdom of our God, and the power of His Christ" (Revelation 12:9, 10).

In the dim light of this apocalyptic mystery we can begin to distinguish more clearly the nature of our rebirth in baptism, that is the beginning of our spiritual lives. Mary and the Church are at work in every soul. All the time Christ on earth is being born, attacked and yet glorified. Yet all this lies hidden behind a humiliating exterior. But it is all there in reality, the new birth into eternity, the sun of the risen Lord. Let us therefore look to her, the noble Lady, our Mother Mary, our mother the Church: let us turn lovingly to the sorrowful mother of our life in Christ. Even Luther from his Catholic days had a touching and warmhearted love for the Blessed Mother, the Church, as is shown in the delicate thought of his hymn to the woman of Revelation:

> *Sie ist mir lieb, die werte Magd,*
> *und kann ihr nicht vergessen,*
> *Lob, Ehr und Zucht man von ihr sagt:*
> *Sie hat mein Herz besessen.*[189]

> She is my love, the noble Maid,
>   Forget her can I never,
> Whatever honor men have paid,
>   My heart she has for ever!

Let us therefore similarly be ready to love and praise the Church, as we do so frequently in our familiar hymns to Mary. For she still suffers pain, because we are sinful and imperfect. She is still dying like the waning moon moving towards the sun. "Truly is the Church still in the world, journeying in the flesh. She is still hidden in the tomb, her light is still hidden from the world. Therefore we are ready to sing of her death, since her death covers the dawn of everlasting life in Christ." But in the end this woman also will be taken up to the throne of God, following her child, and we shall go with her, because we are in Christ Jesus. "In the end we shall all be taken up, from death into life, from sickness into strength, from weakness into glory, from the narrow bonds of time into the wide freedom of eternity."[190]

Thus is Mary, and with her the Church, our consolation in suffering in our spiritual lives, which here on earth seem to be but daily dying; our assurance also of the bright morning of eternity to come, of which already in our hearts we can discern the faintest dawn. Yes, indeed we are already clothed with the sun, and the moon of passing things is already under our feet, "until the day dawn, and the day-star arise in our hearts" (2 Peter 1:19).

As long as it is still night, let us look to the woman with the moon under her feet, for in her all is done, that with us is still to come. For this woman stands for the Church. Yet we can also see in her the Blessed Mary, for she is the mother of the Church, since she gave birth to Him who is the head of the Church.[191]

Chapter Eleven

Queen Assumed into Heaven

We have reached the last stage of our inquiry into the mysteries which our holy mother the Church presents to us concerning our Mother Mary. It is now for us to raise our eyes to the glory that surrounds the mother of our Lord at her entry into everlasting glory, a mystery which has occupied the Church's thought in recent years, and which she has so recently proclaimed as being part of her dogmatic teaching.[192] In so doing the Church has only once more proclaimed the close connection between herself and the Virgin Mary, for in the mystery of the Assumption we have a foreshadowing of what is to come for the whole Church, and what had in fact already been fulfilled in our Lord, "the firstfruits of them that sleep" (1 Corinthians 15:20).

Our Lady's Assumption, the final history of the body of the woman who gave birth to God, is therefore not so much an exception to the rule, but much more a fulfilling in advance of what is promised to the whole Mystical Body of Christ. And moreover it is not only promised, but in a sense already realized, albeit for the present only hidden in sacramental terms, since the way back to paradise through the Redemption of the flesh is already open.

The "aeon that is to come" (it is Paul's word: otherwise "the age" or "the world to come") is already here, it is already present reality (Hebrews 6:5 and Ephesians 1:21), since as Saint Paul also tells us, we are among those "upon whom the ends of the world are come" (1 Corinthians 10:11—where the Greek word is the "aeons," i.e. the present world, and all that went before). It is the end of the present world, because by our faith and our baptism, the new world has begun. "The prince of this world" (or "aeon") (1 Corinthians 2:6), even called "the god of this world" (2 Corinthians 4:4), the devil, has already been defeated, since the Word of God became the seed of the woman (Genesis 3:15) and so crushed the serpent's head, and since the blood of the Redeemer, drawn from His human mother was shed. "Now," as He Himself said "is the judgment of this world: now shall the prince of this world be cast out" (John 12:31). And He said "now," and this is within the Church as the household of God: "For the time has come for the judgment to begin with the household of

God" (1 Peter 4:17, Confraternity text), with the Church throughout her history, though this is but "a little while" (John 16:16), for it is plain in Scripture that the last day and final judgement have begun already. Thus the final glory of Mary, which we recognize with the eye of faith, is a recognition of the final glory of the Church. This indeed sometimes seems very far away in a remotely future time, but then we are often too short-sighted, and need to look close at hand, where we can find the heavenly reality hidden in our everyday lives. Here then we have the supreme instance of the closeness of the mystery of Mary and the Church.

In order to grasp the idea more firmly, let us look again at Revelation:

> And there were given to the woman two wings of a great eagle, that she might fly into the desert unto her place, where she is nourished... away from the serpent.... And the dragon was angry against the woman, and went to make war with the rest of her seed, who keep the commandments of God, and have the testimony of Jesus Christ (Revelation 12:14, 17).

It is at once plain that this applies to the mother that is the Church, taken away into heavenly solitude, yet still fighting the diabolical battle waged against "the rest of her seed," since the dragon's war against her own child "who was to rule all nations with an iron rod" (Revelation 12:3) was frustrated. But the

Fathers of the early Church see in this woman, who is taken out of this world, a symbol also of Mary, the Mother of Jesus; and she, being herself a symbol of the Church struggling towards her final glory, has shown the way by having fulfilled in her own body what for the Church is still in promise, namely the complete victory over Satan and the regaining of the life of paradise, which Eve had forgone through succumbing to the devil's temptation.

Thus in the fourth century Ephrem the Syrian in one of his sermons imagines Mary speaking: "The child whom I carried took me by his eagle's wings and carried me up through the sky; and a voice said to me: 'The heights and the depths which thou seest, shall all belong to thy child!'"[193] For this mystery of the glory of Mary's body is the beginning of the glory of the Church. And we can never appreciate the thought of the early Christians, unless we remind ourselves continually that for them the picture of Mary and the picture of the Church are mutually transparent, and are constantly seen as one. Ephrem considers this in the previous sermon:

> Mary is saying to Jesus: "Shall I call Thee my son? Or my brother, my spouse or my Lord? For Thou hast given birth to Thy mother: rebirth through water. But truly I am Thy sister: from the seed of David like Thee. And truly I am Thy mother, for I conceived Thee in my womb. Thy bride am I, for Thou hast paid the price with Thy death, Thy

daughter in rebirth through Thy baptism. The son of the Most High came and rested within me, and I became His mother. Born of me, He in turn has given me rebirth, for He has clothed His mother with a new garment: He has absorbed His own flesh into Himself, and her He has clothed with the sunshine of Himself."[194]

Here the two pictures are so closely woven into one another that they cannot be separated: the Mother of God in glory has been "born again," for the mystery of rebirth by baptism (which belongs to the Church) is fulfilled in the glory of Mary's body, united to the risen Lord. And in a sense, for mankind the Resurrection of the body is a "birthday." For our Lady this is already complete, in virtue of the redeeming blood of Christ, which she had prepared. And this is a symbol of the Redemption and glory of the Church.

The early Fathers were constantly meditating on the woman with the eagle's wings, in the sense of both Mary and the Church. The Mother of God is also the *Foederis Arca*, the ark of the covenant, in which God Himself came to rest, and this sacred vessel must needs be taken to its proper resting-place in heaven, following the risen Lord. And then the verse of the psalm sprang to their lips: "Arise, O Lord, into Thy resting-place: Thou and the ark which Thou hast sanctified" (Psalm 131:8). Thus the Greek liturgy sings on the Feast of the Assumption: "Come hither, all who love this festival, come let us dance and sing, come let us weave to the

Church a garland of song: for today the ark of God's presence has come to rest!"[195] And the piety of Saint Thomas Aquinas interprets this passage of the psalms of our Lady's Assumption.[196] When the Church celebrates the Assumption, she is celebrating her own final glory.

According to yet another interpretation of the old theology, Mary is the moon, *luna sancta*, who now on the day of her entrance to heaven waxes and wanes no more, but shines forever with the light of her sun. Yet here again is the symbol of the Church, which the Fathers frequently called the sacred moon, for her shining signifies her return to the sunshine of Christ in the final Resurrection of the body.[197] This is a new life, like the youth of the eagle, shining with the light of Christ, the sun of eternal glory: all these images recur when the Fathers speak of the everlasting youth of the Church. Augustine was once preaching about the Church and said:

> On that day, when she will be taken up in the brightness of the Resurrection with Christ, to be queen, then her "youth shall be renewed like the eagle's" (Psalm 102:5). Then she will soar to the height as before and the Resurrection will be perfected in her. And we have an image of this in the moon, waning and finally dying, only to be reborn and grow to the fullness of light. Behold, there is the symbol of our Resurrection.[198]

Indeed we can see in Mary what is to come for the Church: in the end it will be "as before," namely when

Adam and Eve possessed paradise at the beginning. So it will be at the Resurrection, for Jesus and Mary are already preparing for us the new paradise, that is the Church in glory.[199]

And here there opens up a further question, already indicated in the words of Revelation with which we began. Mary, the woman with eagle's wings, has already reached her resting-place, and yet Satan is still making war on "the rest of her seed." The Church is in a true sense already in glory, for the last day and the judgment are already here. But at the same time the Church in her members on earth is still treading the ground in pain and in danger. There is, however, a powerful but mysterious influence of the Church in heaven upon the Church on earth, of Mary upon her children in danger, of the risen Christ upon His still imperfect body.

And here we touch upon a doctrine which is intimately connected with that of the Assumption of our Lady, namely the doctrine of her universal mediation of graces. How often this doctrine is misunderstood, by a narrow-minded supposition that it could injure that central treasure of our faith that is the single mediation of the "one mediator of God and men, the man Christ Jesus" (1 Timothy 2:5)! No, we can only understand it aright in the context of the mystical and symbolic place of Mary in the Church. Pope Pius X, entirely in line with the thought of the Fathers, explained this as follows:

Everyone knows that the great woman of Revelation represents the Virgin Mary, who without blemish gave birth to our Head. But the Apostle continues: "Being with child, she cried travailing in birth and was in pain to be delivered." John therefore saw the holy Mother of God, who indeed already possessed eternal beatitude, nevertheless in pain at a mysterious birth. What birth was this? It was indeed our own birth, for we are still in exile and in a state of being born for the perfect love of God and for everlasting happiness. And the woman's pain also symbolizes the Virgin's love, because of which she labors with unceasing prayer from her place in heaven, to fill up the number of the elect.[200]

If therefore we place Mary's mediation, extending over the whole Church—"the rest of her seed"—in the context of the mystery of her identification with the Church, we can see at once that it cannot involve any diminishing of the immediacy and unique position of Christ's mediation, or the least diminishing of the transmission of grace through the sacraments by the Church herself: for Mary is forever the "handmaid of the Lord" and forever the "mother of the Church."

There is therefore no ground whatever for thinking that Mary's position through the privilege of her mediation in any way detracts from the grace within the Church or from the special place of the divine Redeemer in the work of salvation. There is only one mediation of grace: and what appears in mankind as the reception in a creaturely way of an influx of grace from Christ, appears in Mary as a readiness to receive and the power to undertake her motherly task. She is always present within the Church, and her position is expressed in the title "Mother of divine Grace," since from her flows blessing upon the whole Church.[201]

Thus we can begin to penetrate the impenetrable mystery of the Church that is at once glorious and suffering, through understanding the position of Mary. The Church here is still surrounded by dangers from Satan, and these dangers we have often seen with our own eyes. Yet she is already glorified, and every day her members enter the glory of Christ and His mother. And in her life on earth she is daily fulfilling the mystery of the Incarnation, since Christ our Lord was at one and the same time walking the earth and in possession of the vision of God. "We are sons of God even now, and what we shall be hereafter, has not been made known as yet" (1 John 3:2, Knox). Our Lady was able to understand these two things in her son, and the Church can learn to do so from her. Thus Ephrem the Syrian imagines her as saying:

When I look at Thee from without, and can cast my loving eyes upon Thee, my spirit contemplates what is hidden within Thee. With my eyes I see the form of Adam, while within Thee I see the Father dwelling in Thee. To me alone hast Thou granted the glory of both visions. And may the Church also, like Thy mother, come to see Thee both visible and invisible![202]

The vision of the Lord in glory: this is the goal of all her pilgrimage through her painful history and the purification of her persecutions. She must become like to Mary. When the Church sacramentally gives birth to her children in baptism, she is in fact rising to the blessed desert of solitude with God. With her eagle's wings she rises above this fallen world. For Mary this is all complete: for us, with the human nature which we share with her, it is yet to come.

There is an Armenian hymn for the Feast of the Assumption, which says: "Today the choirs of fiery spirits look upon our own nature, made of clay, and tremble."[203] The theology of heaven among the Russians has preserved this profound insight, derived from the Fathers of the Eastern Church. "High in heavenly glory stands the Virgin Mother of the human race: she has sanctified the whole world of nature, and in her and through her all things shall be gloriously transformed."[204]

The same Russian theology has found an expression of this oneness of the vision of Mary and of the Church in the ikons of the divine wisdom, which are found everywhere in Russia on the example of the great ikon on the wall of the altar in the Church of the Divine Wisdom at Novgorod. The winged female figure of the divine wisdom is enthroned upon the starry circle of the cosmos. Above her is a medallion representing the Logos made man, and on either side are the figures which symbolize the old and new Revelations, John the Baptist and Mary the Mother of Christ. On the top of all is a representation of the everlasting liturgy of heaven performed by the ministry of six angels. Whatever were the origins of this ikon, later Russian mysticism has seen in the figure of the Sophia not only the eternal Word of God, but the whole content, within the Logos from all eternity, of the work of salvation, which through Mary and the Church is to transform all things into the original glory.

The figure of the holy Sophia therefore includes Mary, and within Mary the Church, and within the Church the Christian soul rising slowly through the paths of asceticism and mysticism towards everlasting glory.

Mary, the Church, and the soul: this is the woman with the eagle's wings, soaring to heavenly glory by the power of her assimilation to the all-powerful Logos, for the Logos became man and brought us His revelation, telling us that we on earth will indeed come to share the heavenly liturgy of the fiery angels. A Russian explanation of the ikon in the sixteenth century says:

> The holy Sophia, the divine wisdom, is here the Church of God, and above her is the most pure Mother of God, the lifegiving soul of her who is full of God, the ineffable purity of virginity and the true humility of wisdom. Above her head is Christ,

for the son, the Word of God, is the head of wisdom. Above our Lord is the spread of heaven, for heaven was bowed down when wisdom entered the purity of the Virgin. All who live in purity become like to the Mother of God, for she gave birth to the son, the Word of God, the Lord Jesus Christ. But those also who love virginity conceive words which bear children: that is, they instruct the unwise. And the Precursor, the Baptist, who baptized our Lord, loves them, for it was he who showed the way to virginity and taught men the life of penance. The two figures rest their feet upon a stone, for "upon this rock I will build My Church."

In the instructions for ikon-painting of the school of Stroganov, the explanation is similar:

Of the ikon of the holy Sophia, the divine wisdom, to be painted according to the prototype that is venerated at the great shrine of Novgorod: This is the Church of God, the Sophia, the most pure Virgin Mother of God, that is the soul of the virgins among mankind, the purity of ineffable virginity, and the true humility of wisdom.[205]

Is there not here also a meaning for us, for our own spiritual lives? For us, the words of the Creed which we so often say, "the Resurrection of the body and life everlasting," are being fulfilled within the womb of the Church, for she is both still in the dimness of this world and at the same time flooded with the heavenly light of the Resurrection. To us are given the eagle's wings of the Virgin Church, so that "by the Church's teaching we can avoid the devil, and day by day rise towards our heavenly home."[206] "Ever new and like the eagle, we should rise to the blessed solitude of a quiet and peaceful spirit,"[207] coming home to the "blessed rest," of which a medieval mystic speaks when explaining this verse of Revelation.[208]

And so we reach the end of our study of the mystery of Mary and the Church, and conclude with a beautiful passage from one of the Latin Fathers of the fifth century, which compares the two great women, Mary and the Church, who are one in Christ, and one with us, since "the Virgin Mary has become the Church and every believing soul":[209]

> Let the Church of Christ rejoice, for she like Mary has been graced by the power of the Holy Spirit and has become the mother of a divine child. Let us once more compare these two mothers: each of them through giving birth strengthens our faith in the child of the other.
>
> Upon Mary came in mysterious stillness the shadow of the Holy Spirit, and the Church becomes a mother through the outpouring of the Holy Spirit at baptism.
>
> Mary without blemish gave birth to her son, and the Church washes away every blemish in those she brings to birth.
>
> Of Mary was born He who was from the beginning, of the Church is reborn that which from the beginning was nothing.[210]

The references to Patristic texts are of the usual type, to Migne PG (*Patrologia Graeca*) or PL (*Patrologia Latina*). Some references to Greek texts are given as GCS (*Die griechischen christlichen Schriftsteller der ersten drei Jahrhunderte*) otherwise known as CB (*Corpus Berolinense*), and some references to Latin texts as CSEL (*Corpus Scriptorum ecclesiasticorum latinorum*), which is sometimes referred to as CV (*Corpus Vindobenense*). The translator has ventured to add (in square brackets) a number of references to Migne, which were not in the original book.

The translator has also included the Latin text of the lines from the *Carmen Paschale*, and the verse of the hymn *Fonte prolem salutari*, neither of which was originally printed. He has also retained the German text of the verses by Tauler and Luther as they were given in the book.

Biblical quotations are from the Douay version, unless otherwise indicated.

Notes

FOREWORD

1. *Evangelii concordantis Expositio* (ed. Moesinger, p. 49).

2. Isaac of Stella, Sermo 51 on the Assumption (PL 194, 1863).

CHAPTER 1

3. R. Guardini, *Das Erwachen der Kirche in der Seele:* in *Hochland* 19 (1922), pp. 257-67.

4. On the speculative side an important contribution is that of O. Semmelroth, *Urbild der Kirche: organischer Aufbau des Mariengeheimnisses* [A symbol of the Church, the development of Marian doctrine], Würzburg, 1950. On the Patristic side, see J. B. Terrien, *La Mère de Dieu et la Mere des hommes d'après les Pères et la Théologie*, II, Paris, 1902, pp. 1-27: *Parallèle entre Marie et l'Église*. See also H. Rahner, *Mater Ecclesia: Lobpreis der Kirche aus dem ersten Jahrtausend*, [The Praise of the Church during the first millennium], Einsiedeln, 1944, pp. 11ff; and S. Tromp, *Ecclesia Sponsa Virgo Mater*, in *Gregorianum* 18 (1937), pp. 3-29.

5. Sermo 25, 8 (ed. Morin, Rome 1930, p. 163).

6. Commentary on the Canticle (*Texte and Untersuchungen* 23, 2, Leipzig, 1903, pp. 32f).

7. Fragment from the Great Ode (GCS Hippolytus I, 2, p. 83).

8. *Adv. Haer.* III, 10, 2-3 (PG 7, 873f).

9. The Blessings of Moses 15 (*Texte und Untersuchungen* 26, I, p. 66).

10. Hymn 5 on the Birth of the Lord in the flesh, verse 5 (ed. Lamy, II, p. 486).

11. *De institutione virginis* 14, 87 (PL 16, 326f).

12. *Hexaemeron* (PG 89, 1072).

13. *Acta Archelai* (GCS Hegemonius, p. 81).

14. Homily 4 (PG 77, 996).

15. Commentary on Luke I, 2 (PL 92, 330).

16. Commentary on Ephesians 5:32 (PL 26, 535).

17. *Confessions* IV, 12, 19 (CSEL 33, p. 79). [PL 32, 701.]

18. Epiphanius of Salamis, *Panarion* III, 2, 78 (PG 42, 728-9).

CHAPTER 2

19. Sermo 102 (Mai I, 212).

20. Irenaeus, *Adv. Haer.* III, 23, 7 (PG 7, 964).

21. Ibid. V, 21, 1 (PG 7, 1179).

22. Hymn 2 on the Birth of the Lord, v. 31 (ed. Lamy, II, p. 455f).

23. *Enarr. in Psalmos* 103:6 (PL 37, 1381).

24. Bruno of Asti, Commentary on Genesis (PL 164, 169).

25. *Passio Andreae* 5 (Lipsius-Bonnet, II, 1, p. 11).

26. Cf. Ps-Ambrose, Sermo 6, 7 (PL 17, 616); Adamantius, Dialogue V, 8 (GCS, p. 191).

27. Rupert of Deutz, Commentary on the Canticle 5 (PL 168, 912).

28. Commentary on the Canticle I (GCS VIII, p. 99).

29. Justus of Urgel (PL 67, 980); Bede (PL 91, 1155); Haymo (PL 117, 327); Bruno of Asti (PL 164, 1263).

30. Honorius, Commentary on the Canticle 5 (PL 172, 435).

31. Commentary on Luke II, 7 (CSEL 32, 4, p. 45).

32. *Tract. in Joann.* 57, 4 (PL 35, 1791).

33. Mozarabic Liturgy (Férotin p. 54).

34. Ps-Jerome, *Epistola ad Paulam* 9 (PL 30, 127, 132).

35. Homily 2 on "Missus est" (PL 183, 62).

36. *Adv. Marcionem* II, 4 (CSEL 47, p. 338). [PL 2, 289.]

37. Methodius of Philippi, *Symposion* 8, 5 (GCS p. 86). [PG 18, 145.]

38. Ps-Ambrose (= Berengaud), Commentary on the Apocalypse, IV, 3, 4 (PL 17, 876).

CHAPTER 3

39. De Virginibus I, 6, 31 (PL 16, 197).

40. *Epideixis* I, 32-33 (Weber pp. 23f).

41. *Adv. Haer*. IV, 33, 4 (PG 7, 1074).

42. Commentary on Luke IV, 7 (PL 15, 1614).

43. Cf. C. Passaglia, *De Ecclesia Christi* I (Rome 1853), pp. 78ff.

44. Eusebius, Church History IV, 22, 4 (PG 20, 380).

45. Epistle to Diognetus 12, 8 (Bihlmayer p. 149). [PG 2, 1185.]

46. *Ode of Solomon* 33 (Hennecke, pp. 465f).

47. *De catholicae ecclesiae unitate* 6 (PL 4, 502f).

48. Sermo 178, 4 (PL 38, 1005).

49. Sermo 341, 5 (PL 39, 1496).

50. Commentary on John 3 (PL 92, 675).

51. Sermo 213, 7 (PL 38, 1064).

52. Christmas Sermon 2, 2 (PL 54, 195f).

53. *De Virginibus* I, 3, 13 and 5, 22 (PL 16, 192 and 195).

54. Ibid. II, 2, 6 (PL 16, 208).

55. Tract I, 8 (Morin, p. 447).

56. Sermo 195, 2 (PL 38, 1013).

CHAPTER 4

57. *Mystici Corporis* (June 29, 1943), in AAS 35 [1943], p. 231.

58. *Lux veritatis* (December 25, 1931), in AAS 25 [1931], p. 512.

59. *Mystici Corporis* (AAS 35 [1943], p. 226).

60. *De Antichristo* 61 (GCS Hippolytus I, 2, pp. 41f). [PG 10, 780f.]

61. Cf. H. Rahner, *Die Gottesgeburt*, in *Zeitschrift für kath. Theologie* 59 [1935], pp. 352 ff.

62. Homily on Luke 12 (GCS Origen IX, p. 84).

63. Commentary on the Canticle, Prologue (GCS Origen VIII, p. 74).

64. *De sanguisuga* 8, 2 (GCS Methodius, p. 486).

65. *Symposion* 8, 11 (GCS Methodius, p. 93). [PG 18, 153.]

66. Ibid. 8, 8 (GCS Methodius, p. 90). [PG 18, 149.]

67. *Constitutiones Apostolicae* II, 61, 5 (Funk, I, p. 117). [PG I, 750f.]

68. *Hexaemeron* 12 (PG 89, 1072).

69. Tract I, 8 (Morin, p. 447).

70. Sermo 25, 8 (Morin, p. 163).

71. *Enarr. in Psalmos* 127:12 (PL 37, 1685).

72. Easter Homily 3 (PL 67, 1048).

73. Homily 9 on the Apocalypse (PL 35, 2434).

74. Commentary on the Apocalypse 12 (PL 17, 877).

75. On the Apocalypse III, 12 (PL 117, 1081).

76. Commentary on the Apocalypse 12, 5 (ed. Borgnet, 38, p. 656).

77. *Expositio in Lucam* 1, 2 (PL 92, 330).

78. *Die Mysterien des Christentums* VII, 79 (Mainz 1931), p. 512.

79. *Paidagogos* I, 6, 42 (GCS Clement, I, p. 115).

CHAPTER 5

80. Sermo 25, 8 (Morin, p. 163).

81. *Allegoriae* 139 (PL 83, 117).

82. A. Paredi, *I Prefazi Ambrosiani* (Milan 1937), p. 201.

83. *De sancta virginitate* 6 (PL 40, 399).

84. *Analecta Hymnica* 51 (1908), p. 148.

85. Carmen, 25, 155-83 (CSEL 30, pp. 243f). Cf. H. Rahner, *Mater Ecclesia*, p. 47.

86. Sermo 26, 2 (PL 54, 213).

87. Gelasian Sacramentary, Easter Preface (ed. Muratori, p. 572; PL 74, 1112). Cf. *Mater Ecclesia*, p. 66.

88. Sermo 2 (PL 96, 252).

89. PL 169, 155.

90. Hymn on the Lord's mysteries 34, 1 (ed. Lamy, II, p. 822).

91. Commentary on John II (PL 169, 285).

92. Commentary on John I, 4, 23 (PG 14, 32).

93. *Evangelii concordantis expositio* (ed. Moesinger, p. 134).

94. Commentary on Luke 10, 34 (PL 15, 1838).

95. Commentary on Luke 7, 5 (PL 15, 1700).

96. Cf. *Mater Ecclesia*, p. 17, note 21.

97. Scivias II, 6 (PL 197, 507); cf. *Mater Ecclesia*, p. 55.

98. *Liber de gloria Filii hominis* 10 (PL 194, 1105).

99. Encyclical *Adjutricem populi* (Sept. 5, 1895), ed. Herder, V, 1, p. 7.

100. *De Virginibus*, I, 6, 31 (PL 16, 197).

101. Anastasius of Sinai, *Hexaemeron* 12 (PL 89, 1074); cf. *Mater Ecclesia*, p. 114.

CHAPTER 6

102. *Adv. Haer*. IV, 33, 4 (PG 7, 1074).

103. Ibid. IV, 33, 11 (PG 7, 1080).

104. Commentary on Luke II, 57 (PL 15, 1573).

105. Hymn 3 on the Birth of the Lord, v. 5 (ed. Lamy, II, pp. 464f).

106. *Tract. in Joannem* II, 15 (PL 35, 1395).

107. Text in E. Diehl, *Inscriptiones latinae christianae veteres* (1926), p. 289.

108. Sermo 24, 3 (PL 54, 206).

109. Sermo 25, 5 (PL 54, 211).

110. *Analecta Hymnica* 51 (1908), p. 112. [Father Rahner's beautiful German translation, which has also influenced the above version, deserves to be quoted:

> *Aus dem Taufquell weiss und lieblich*
> *und mit Chrismaduft gesalbt,*
> *führt die mütterliche Jungfrau*
> *ihre Kinder in das Licht,*
> *die das hehre Kind des Vaters,*
> *Christus, für den Himmel zeugt.* Tr.]

111. Sermo 8 (PL 162, 570).

112. Encyclical *Adjutricem populi* (Sept. 5, 1895), ed. Herder, V, 1, p. 8.

113. Homily 4 (PG 77, 992).

114. Mozarabic Liturgy (Férotin, p. 250).

115. Tract 33 (PL 11, 479).

116. Sermo 117 (PL 52, 521).

117. Ps-Augustine, Sermo 135 (PL 39, 1012).

118. Blessing of the Font at the Easter Vigil.

CHAPTER 7

119. Cf. H. Rahner, *Geburt aus Jem Herzen* [Birth from the heart], in *Gloria Dei* 4 (1949). pp. 89-99.

120. Homily on Exodus 10, 4 (GCS Origen VI, p. 250). [PG 12, 373.]

121. *Selecta in Genesim* (PG 12, 124).

122. *Symposion* 8, 8 (GCS Methodius, p. 90). [PG 18, 149.]

123. *De caeco et Zachaeo* 4 (PG 59, 605).

124. *De Virginitate* 2 (PG 46, 324).

125. Ibid. 13 (PG 46, 380).

126. Commentary on the Canticle 4 (PG 44, 828).

127. *De Virginitate* 4, 20 (PL 16, 271).

128. Commentary on Luke X, 24-25 (CSEL 32, 4, p. 464f). [PL 15, 1810.]

129. Sermo 191, 4 (PL 38, 1011).

130. Sermo 192, 2 (PL 38, 1012).

131. Mozarabic Liturgy (Férotin, p. 54).

132. Homily 3 on the Gospels (PL 76, 1086).

133. Commentary on Mt. 4, 12 (PL 107, 937).

134. Haymo of Halberstadt, Commentary on the Apocalypse III, 12 (PL 117, 1081).

135. Commentary on the Apocalypse IV, 1 (PL 196, 799).

CHAPTER 8

136. Cf. H. Rahner, *Mater Ecclesia* (Einsiedeln 1944), pp. 27f; and *Die Kirche als das starke Weib* [The Church as the valiant woman], in *Licht des Lebens* 6 (1947), pp. 3f.

137. Adam of Perseigne, Sermo 5 (PL 211, 733ff).

138. Ancoratus 101 (GCS Epiphanius I, p. 122) [PG 43, 200].

139. Hymn 2 to the Virgin Mary, v. 5 (ed. Lamy, II, p. 525).

140. In *Bibliothek der Kirchenväter, Syrische Dichter*, p. 287; cf. T. Livius, *Die allerseligeste Jungfrau bei den Vätern der ersten sechs Jahrhunderte* [The B.V. and the fathers of the first 600 years], (Trier 1907) II, pp. 40f.

141. Quoted from S. Beissel, *Geschichte der Verehrung Marias in Deutschland während des Mittelalters* [History of medieval German devotion to our Lady] (Freiburg 1909), p. 226. [The four verses of this carol will be found in many German carol books. Tr.]

142. *Opus imperfectum in Matthaeum*, Homily 23 (PG 56, 755).

143. Sermo 37 (PL 38, 221 and 225).

144. Sermo 5 (PL 211, 734).

145. Salonius of Geneva, *Expositio mystica in parabolas Salomonis* (PL 53, 989).

146. Commentary on Luke VIII, 10-12 (CSEL 32, 4, 396f). [PL 15, 1768.]

147. Sermo 27, 20 (PL 38, 235).

CHAPTER 9

148. A. Boudou, *Actes des Apôtres* (Verbum Salutis VII), Paris 1933, p. 15.

149. *Glossa ordinaria* on Acts 1:14 (PL 113, 429).

150. *De Actibus Apostolorum* I, 57-68 (PL 68, 95f).

151. *De sancta Virginitate* 3 (PL 40, 398).

152. Saint Augustine, Sermo 225, 4 (PL 38, 1074).

153. Bruno of Segni, Commentary on Luke I, 7 (PL 165, 355).

154. Homily on Luke, 20 (GCS Origen IX, p. 134).

155. Theodoret of Ancyra (PG 77, 1395).

156. *De Civitate Dei* XVII, 24 (PL 41, 559).

157. Rupert of Deutz, *De operibus Spiritus Sancti* I, 9 and 23 (PL 167, 1578 and 1630).

158. Scholion of Metaphrastes (A. Mai, *Script. Vet. Nova Collectio* IX, p. 656).

159. Ps-Gregory Thaumaturgus (PG 10, 1169).

160. As in a carving of the ninth century in Paris. Cf. A. Goldschmidt, *Die Elfenbeinskulpturen der karolingischen Zeit* [The ivory carvings of the Carolingian age], I, Fig. 86.

161. *Carmen paschale* V, 357-60 (PL 19, 742).

162. Cf. H. Schrade, *Zur Ikonographie der Himmelfahrt Christi* [Towards an Iconography of Christ's ascension] (Warburg Library lectures 1928-9), pp. 156ff.

163. Rupert of Deutz, *De operibus Spiritus Sancti* I, 8 (PL 167, 1577).

164. *De glorificatione Trinitatis* VII, 5 and 6 (PL 169, 146f).

165. Commentary on Luke II, 54 (PL 15, 1572).

166. Ibid. II, 26 (PL 15, 1561).

167. *Mystici Corporis* (AAS 35 [1943], p. 248).

CHAPTER 10

168. *De Antichristo* 61 (GCS I, 2, p. 41) [PG 10, 780].

169. Coptic Fragment on the Apocalypse I (GCS I, 2, pp. 207f).

170. *De Antichristo* 61 (GCS I, 2, p. 41). [PG 10, 750f.]

171. Ps-Ambrose (= Berengaud), *In Apoc. Expos.* (PL 17, 875).

172. *Symposion* 8, 5 (GCS Methodius, pp. 86f) [PG 18, 145]; cf. H. Rahner, *Mater Ecdesia* (Einsiedeln 1944), p. 117.

173. *Symposion* 8, 7 (GCS Methodius, p. 89f). [PG 18, 148f.]

174. Cf. Epiphanius of Salamis (PG 42, 716); Andrew of Caesarea (PG 106, 319); Arethas (PG 106, 660).

175. Ps-Augustine, *De Symbolo ad Catechumenos*, Sermos IV, 1 (PL 40, 661).

176. Commentary on the Apocalypse V, 12 (PL 100, 1152).

177. *Expositio in Apoc.* III, 12 (PL 117, 1080f).

178. Commentary on the Apocalypse VII, 12 (PL. 169, 1043).

179. *Expositio in Apoc.* III, 12 (PL 117, 1081).

180. Cf. H. Rahner, *Mysterium Lunae: Ein Beitrag zur Kirchentheologie der Väterzeit* [A study of the theology of the Church in patristic times], in *Zeitschrift für kath. Theologie* 63 (1939), pp. 311ff.

181. *Glaphyra in Genesim* 6 (PG 69, 329); cf. *Mater Ecclesia*, pp. 99f.

182. *Glaphyra in Genesim* 4 (PG 69, 224f); cf. *Mysterium Lunae*, p. 345.

183. *Explanatio Apoc*. II, 12 (PL 93, 165).

184. Coptic Fragment on the Apocalypse 12, 5 (GCS I, 2, p. 208).

185. *Symposion* 8, 8 (GCS Methodius, p. 90). [PG 18, 149.]

186. Ps-Augustine, Homily 9 on the Apocalypse (PL 35, 2434); cf. H. Rahner, *Die Gottesgeburt*, in *Zeitschrift für kath. Theologie* 59 (1935), pp. 398f.

187. On Apoc. 12 (Venice edition 1754, vol. VII, p. 401).

188. Commentary on the Apocalypse (ed. Vives [Paris 1866], vol. XII, p. 235).

189. Luther's Works: Weimar ed. 35, 254ff., 462f.; Buchwald ed. 8, 73f; Philadelphia ed. 7, 307. The hymn *Sie ist mir lieb* is ascribed to the year 1535.

190. Cyril of Alexandria (PG 69, 225); cf. *Mater Ecclesia*, p. 100.

191. Ps-Ambrose (PL 17, 876).

CHAPTER 11

192. The translator has slightly modified the opening sentences, since they were originally written while the proclamation of the Assumption as a dogma was still being awaited.

193. Sermo 12 (*Opera syriace et latine* [Rome 1740], II, p. 430).

194. Sermo II (Ibid., p. 429).

195. Vespers for August 15 (Roman edition 1901, p. 409).

196. *Expositio in Salutationem Angelicam* (*Opera* Parma ed., vol. XVI, p. 134).

197. Theodore the Studite (PG 99, 720); cf. H. Rahner, *Mysterium Lunae* III, *Die strahlende Kirche*: in *Zeitschrift für kath. Theologie* 64 (1940), pp. 121-31.

198. *Enarr. in Psalmos* 102, 9 (PL 37, 1323).

199. William of Auvergne, Sermo I on the Assumption: quoted without further reference by M. Jugie, *La Mort et l'Assomption de la Sainte Vierge* (Rome 1944), p. 381.

200. Encyclical *Ad diem illum*, Feb. 2, 1904 (AAS 36 [1904], pp. 458f).

201. J. Beumer, *Die Analogie Maria-Kirche und ihre Bedeutung für die allgemeine Gnadenvermittlung der Gottesmutter* [The Analogy of Mary and the Church, and its significance for Mary's universal mediation], in *Theologie und Seelsorge*, August 1943, p. 44.

202. Sermo II (*Opera syriace et latine*, II, p. 429).

203. Quoted by Jugie, in *La Mort et l'Assomption*, p. 309.

204. S. Bulgakow, *L'Orthodoxie* (Paris 1932), pp. 166f.

205. A.M. Ammann, *Darstellung und Deutung der Sophia im vorpetrinischen Russland* [The representation and significance of the Sophia in pre-Petrine Russia] in *Orientalia Christiana periodica* 4 (1938), pp. 148-54.

206. Ps-Ambrose (PL 17, 880).

207. Bede (PL 93, 168).

208. Rupert of Deutz (PL 169, 1061).

209. Hildebert of Le Mans (PL 171, 609).

210. Ps-Caesarius of Arles (PL 67, 1068).

Index

A NOTE ON THE TYPE

The text is set in Sabon Next, a redesigned version of Sabon. The original Sabon, by the noted 20th-century typographer Jan Tschihold, is considered one of the most beautiful Garamond variations, and Tschihold's most important creation.

Sabon Next, created by Jean François Porchez in 2002, reflects the best in contemporary digitized typeface design. Classic, elegant, and extremely legible, Sabon Next captures the essence of the original Sabon, as well as its Garamond ancestors, while at the same time conveying the weight and visual texture of traditional metal fonts, a value often lost in the first generation of digitized fonts.

ABOUT THE AUTHOR

Father Hugo Rahner, a Jesuit theologian, was born in Baden, Germany in 1900. He studied in Holland, Innsbruck, and Bonn; he was on the theological faculty and later became the Rector of the University of Innsbruck. He retired due to illness in 1964, and died in 1968. He is the author of many books, several of which have appeared in English, including *Ignatius the Theologian*, and *Church and State in Early Christianity*.

ABOUT THE TRANSLATOR

Born in Cambridge in 1910, Father Sebastian Bullough entered the Dominican order and was ordained a priest in 1937. The scholarly son of scholarly parents, he taught at Oxford and Cambridge and, in addition to his work as a translator, authored several books and many articles. He died in 1967.

Zaccheus Press

Zaccheus Press is a small Catholic press devoted to publishing fine books for all readers seeking a deeper understanding of the Catholic faith.

To learn more about Zaccheus Press, please visit our webpage. We welcome your comments, questions, and suggestions.

www.zaccheuspress.com

And behold, there was a rich man named Zaccheus, who was the chief among the tax collectors. And he sought to see Jesus, but could not because of the crowd, for he was short of stature. So he ran ahead and climbed up into a sycamore tree to see Him, for He was going to pass that way.

—Luke 19:2-4